LEN MUNSIL
PRESIDENT, ARIZONA CHRISTIAN UNIVERSITY

TRANSFORMING CULTURE *with* TRUTH

SECOND EDITION

Transforming Culture with Truth
Second Edition

Copyright © Arizona Christian University Press, 2020

All rights reserved under International and Pan-American Copyright Conventions. Reproductions or translation of any part of this work beyond that permitted by section 107 or 108 of the 1976 United States Copyright Act is unlawful without prior permission from Arizona Christian University Press.

Arizona Christian University Press is the book-publishing division of Arizona Christian University, a private Christian university in Glendale, Arizona, that provides a biblically-integrated, liberal arts education equipping graduates to serve the Lord Jesus Christ in all aspects of life, as leaders of influence and excellence. Arizona Christian University exists to educate and equip followers of Christ to tranform culture with truth.

Requests for permissions should be addressed to:

Arizona Christian University Press
1 W. FirestormWay
Glendale, AZ 85306

ISBN 978-1-7357763-5-4

Printed in the United States of America

DEDICATION

This book is first dedicated to the students of Arizona Christian University—past, present and future—and to the Trustees, faculty, staff and ACU community who have embraced this vision to allow God to work through them to transform our decaying culture with biblical truth.

This book is also dedicated to my partner in life and in Kingdom mission, Dr. Tracy Munsil, who was my editor in college when I was 19 and resumed that role for both versions of this book, and to our eight adult children and their spouses—who through their careers and the families they are forming now have the opportunity to continue this transformational Kingdom work for a new generation.

CONTENTS

~

Introduction	7
Arizona Christian University Core Commitments	27
ONE	29
TWO	39
THREE	55
FOUR	71
FIVE	89
SIX	101
SEVEN	109
EIGHT	147
CONCLUSION	157
About the Author	161

INTRODUCTION

∼

Many of our Christian institutions, especially the great Christian liberal arts colleges, come out of a tradition that tilts in the direction of separation from culture. Many are in isolated places where connection to our powerful urban centers is limited. We have often structured our institutions so that our students separate from the world "for a time," as we say, so they may then "enter the world" prepared. This is the ivory tower model. This is the belief that there is something called pure learning....

But I do not buy into these notions. Such a tradition may have been appropriate for another time, but no longer. It seems abundantly clear that ***the gospel calls us into vigorous cultural engagement.*** *Any preparation apart from this core commitment—to engage the culture—neglects the central call of the gospel on our Christian universities. We must engage the culture to change the world. In my opinion, this is the clear and critical direction for the future of the Christian university.*

—Dr. Philip W. Eaton
Former President, Seattle Pacific University, 2011
Engaging the Culture, Changing the World: The Christian University in a Post-Christian World[1]

In spite of the brilliant technological, scientific and medical advances of our time, there is a sickness at the soul of America.

We have forgotten who we are.

More specifically, as Abraham Lincoln warned more than a

century-and-a-half ago, "we have forgotten God"[2] and the central role of biblical Christianity in the formation of America and its foundational institutions—including its universities.

Today those foundations are under attack like never before. Rather than celebrating our history—while recognizing our failure at times to live up to our aspirational principles—we are told to be embarrassed and ashamed.

There are essentially two views of America and American history right now, and it seems every battle being fought in our culture—in politics, business, entertainment, education and more—is rooted in these contrasting views. One view recognizes that our nation, though flawed, was founded on truths that come from God and should be celebrated. The other view, which is rapidly increasing in our culture today, holds a counterfeit, revisionist perspective that almost requires us to tear everything down and start over.

This view is on the increase because generations of students have been lied to about our history and taught to hate God, hate themselves and hate their country. Arrogant in their ignorance, in the name of attacking injustice, they seek to tear down the very system that taught them about justice and gave them the liberty to speak and protest. And most importantly, the freedom to overcome obstacles, pursue their dreams and determine their own destiny.

But here is the truth that has been lost, and that we must recover: The United States of America, with all of its flaws and failings—because of the biblical principles present at its founding and the virtue of its many God-fearing people through the years—has been the most humane, selfless, peaceful, prosperous, welcoming and just nation in the history of the world.

Not perfect, of course. We have been let down often by the failure of sinful people to live up to our core principles and values, enabling corruption, deprivation of liberty and many injustices, including moral atrocities like slavery and abortion.

But our foundational core biblical principles—the value of every

INTRODUCTION

life, the freedom to pursue God, a separation of powers and limited government in recognition of man's sinful tendency to abuse power, equal justice under law—these have created the best opportunity in human history for people to flourish and live out God's purposes here on earth.

And to be clear, these biblical principles can guide any culture, any people and any nation toward freedom and human flourishing. When the United States has successfully influenced other nations with these principles—when we have been as "a city set on a hill," a model to other nations—their people have benefited as well. To the extent biblical principles guide nations, those nations will be blessed. America is exceptional only because it has so often embraced biblical principles of truth, justice and human rights that many nations don't even pretend to honor.

Every nation of the world—from Bible times to more recent history—has a history and a past. And without exception, those histories are filled with horrific examples of man's inherent sinfulness, leading to wars of conquest, genocides and rampant injustices.

But history today is taught to young people in our country without context. So it is that the one nation that has successfully welcomed and united people from all races and religions and nationalities with its principles of freedom and human rights is now condemned for xenophobia, racism and intolerance. The one nation that has sought to use its influence and at times its armies to advance freedom and liberate people from other nations is now condemned for its international influence. The one nation that has established and enforced principles of equality under the law, enabling people of all races, nationalities and backgrounds to succeed and flourish is now condemned as fundamentally unjust. The one nation every other nation turns to for help when disaster strikes—and that always sends help—is now condemned as selfish and greedy.

This is madness. We have made the perfect the enemy of the good. But we should be capable of making a clear-eyed analysis of our flaws and failings without condemning and repudiating our entire history as a nation.

We have much to learn from our national history. We should celebrate the good, not seek to tear it all down. I'm reminded of the frustrated words of the prophet Jeremiah, unsuccessfully attempting to direct God's people back to the truths from their history:

> Thus says the LORD,
> "Stand by the ways and see and ask for the ancient paths,
> Where the good way is, and walk in it;
> And you will find rest for your souls."
> But they said, "We will not walk in it" (Jeremiah 6:16).

I pray that would not be true for us today—I pray instead that we would look back to our godly heritage, find "where the good way is," then pursue those "ancient paths" and "walk in [them]."

To truly understand the biblical influences that led to the founding of America and to its higher education system, you have to go back before the American Revolution—to the Pilgrims who risked their lives on a perilous ocean crossing to flee religious persecution in Europe in 1620.

While still aboard the *Mayflower*, these Christians agreed to foundational principles for the new community they would form when they went ashore. This document, which became known as the Mayflower Compact, stated they had come to the new world "for the glory of God" and to advance "the Christian faith." They agreed to govern themselves in a "civil body politic" that would frame "just and equal laws" in the best interests of their community. I am descended from five signers of that document.[3]

Ten years later in 1630, before landing on American shores, and while still on their ship, the *Arbella*, John Winthrop delivered a sermon entitled "A Model of Christian Charity." Winthrop, who would be elected governor a year later, essentially challenged the colonists to demonstrate Christian love, to bear each other's burdens and thereby

INTRODUCTION

set an example for the world: "For we must consider that we shall be as a city upon a hill. The eyes of all people are upon us. So that if we shall deal falsely with our God in this work we have undertaken, and so cause Him to withdraw His present help from us, we shall be made a story and a by-word through the world."[4]

Winthrop was referring to the words of Jesus from the Sermon on the Mount, recorded in Matthew 5:14-16: "You are the light of the world. A city set on a hill cannot be hidden... Let your light shine before men in such a way that they may see your good works and glorify your Father who is in heaven."

This vision of the United States of America has been embraced by American leaders across the political spectrum. Democrat President John F. Kennedy used this imagery in a final speech to the Massachusetts legislature in 1961, less than two weeks before his Inauguration as President. Republican President Ronald Reagan used this metaphor as a recurring theme throughout his campaigns and during his presidency. And Democrat President Barack Obama as a young Senator—two years before his election as America's first African-American President—beautifully articulated this vision for American exceptionalism in a Commencement address at the University of Massachusetts in Boston:

> It was right here, in the waters around us, where the American experiment began. As the earliest settlers arrived on the shores of Boston and Salem and Plymouth, they dreamed of building a City upon a Hill. And the world watched, waiting to see if this improbable idea called America would succeed.
>
> For over two hundred years, it has. Not because our dream has progressed perfectly. It hasn't. It has been scarred by our treatment of native peoples, betrayed by slavery, clouded by the subjugation of women, wounded by racism, shaken by war and depression.
>
> Yet, the true test of our union is not whether it's perfect, but

whether we work to perfect it. Whether we recognize our failings, identify our shortcomings, and then rise to meet the challenges of our time....

Now, there may be some who doubt that much has changed—those who doubt that things are better today than they were yesterday. To them I say take a look at this class of 2006.

More than half of you represent the very first member of your family to ever attend college.... I see students that have come here from over 100 different countries, believing like those first settlers that they too could find a home in this City on a Hill—that they too could find success in this unlikeliest of places.[5]

President Obama, like presidents before him, recognized that despite our flaws, the principles of the United States have provided opportunities for advancement unparalleled in the history of the world.

That is why people trapped in oppressive socialist regimes from all over the world will sacrifice almost anything to get to America. If the anti-American activists who believe our nation has always been fundamentally evil and corrupt were correct, people would be fleeing the United States. Instead, they risk their lives to reach what the rest of the world understands is truly a "land of opportunity." For now.

And that's the irony—the activists now seeking to tear down the United States in most cases are promoting the very unbiblical, leftist economic and social policies that the rest of the world is trying to escape.

So, we need to start by remembering who we are, by recovering and re-implementing the biblical foundations that led us to becoming that "city on a hill."

Although many Americans today seem to have fully embraced secularist ideology, America began as a place where virtuous biblical

INTRODUCTION

principles were universally understood to be essential to the American idea of liberty. From the beginning of our nation, colleges and universities were created with that same biblical worldview, and with the expectation that they would produce Christian students of influence, excellence and high moral character.

As Dr. Phillip W. Eaton indicates in his powerful book, *Engaging the Culture, Changing the World: The Christian University in a Post-Christian World*[6], now is not the time for Christian universities to retreat further from the public sphere. More than ever, Christian universities today should focus on preparing leaders who can, by God's grace, provide hope and healing to a wounded culture and to a lost generation.

The leading American institutions of higher learning almost uniformly began with such clear purpose. Just 16 years after the *Mayflower* arrived, America's first university was founded in 1636 for the explicit purpose of training "a literate clergy."[7] Students at Harvard University were governed by "Rules and Precepts" that required reading Scripture twice a day, with students required to report to their instructor about their Bible reading twice a day.

The "Rules and Precepts" stated: "Let every Student be plainly instructed and earnestly pressed to consider well, the maine end of his life and studies, is to know God and Jesus Christ which is eternal life, John 17:3 and therefore to lay Christ in the bottome, as the only foundation of all sound knowledge and Learning."[8] The founders of Harvard believed "All knowledge without Christ was vain."[9]

In the 18th Century, the founders of Yale wrote that "Every student shall consider the main end of his study to wit to know God in Jesus Christ and answerably to lead a Godly, sober life."[10] Requirements for students included:

> All scholars shall live religious, godly and blameless lives according to the rules of God's Word, diligently reading the Holy Scriptures, the fountains of light and truth; and constantly attend upon all the duties of religion, both in

public and secret.

Seeing God is the giver of all wisdom, every scholar, besides private or secret prayer, where we are all bound to ask for wisdom, shall be present morning and evening at public prayer…[11]

Imagine—public prayer was expected twice a day for Yale students—although additional private prayer was assumed! Prayers were focused on seeking wisdom from God. After all, what serious scholar could expect to find wisdom without asking God and without recourse to the truths of the Bible?

That perspective permeated the American colonies and the early days of our nation. Noah Webster, author of the dictionary and founder of historic Amherst College, put it bluntly—"Education is useless without the Bible."[12]

This perspective did not begin with American universities. The first universities in history developed in Europe during medieval times out of Christian monasteries, where the pursuit of knowledge and wisdom was tied directly into the pursuit of God's truth. The Reformation had a profound influence on the direction of universities.

How far universities have fallen from their initial purpose is obvious to any observer of higher education today. Today, a university like Arizona Christian University that holds to biblical truth is often criticized and attacked by a hostile culture.

Having gone through the college selection process eight times with our own children, we were amazed at how even some of the most elite universities marketed themselves. At a time when underage drinking is a major national concern, we heard a paid admissions advisor for one elite, historic college tout how many local bars were within a block or two of campus at a meeting for hundreds of prospective students and their parents. At another college—during a weekend when parents were invited to visit—we were welcomed with rhyming chalk art letting us know that if we left our students there

INTRODUCTION

"for a year, [they would] turn them queer," and informing us that "America was built on racism and genocide." Numerous books have been written by secular scholars regarding the effect on our young people of the destructive "hook-up culture" that is prevalent on most college campuses.

In short, the historic function of a university to teach and train students in the pursuit of God's truth, and the desire for scholars to pray and seek wisdom while attempting to understand the history and meaning of the world and of life in a biblical context—all of that is gone. In its place, partying, sexual immorality and substance abuse—seemingly with the tacit approval of some university leaders. Combining those traumatic experiences with secular, left-wing indoctrination that promotes a false view of the world that either denies the existence of God or is antagonistic to biblical truth is beyond destructive. In too many circumstances, students have borrowed or paid tens or hundreds of thousands of dollars for the privilege of learning irrational and immoral nonsense while undergoing painful experiences that may require years of therapy to overcome.

The consequences of this type of education coming from our universities are increasingly obvious. Our cultural leaders—in the arts, media, business, politics and elsewhere—have often been prepared and equipped with a worldview that can only succeed in tearing down what is true, good and beautiful.

Two Christian leaders I admire recognized the problems with American universities and sought to do something about it. Each played a key role in encouraging and inspiring the decision I made to accept the presidency at Arizona Christian University, and to present a new vision for ACU to be at the forefront of preparing Christian leaders for cultural engagement.

The first is Michael Farris, a founder of the Home School Legal Defense Association (HSLDA) and Patrick Henry College in Purcellville, Virginia, and now serving as President and CEO of Alliance Defending Freedom (ADF). I have been active in conservative

Christian pro-life, pro-family, parental rights and religious freedom issues for several decades, so I had already met him on numerous occasions. When we began thinking about college for our children years ago, we received a tour of Patrick Henry from Michael Farris, who was then its President.

In November of 2006, the day after I lost the general election for Governor of Arizona, Tracy and I decided to get away from Phoenix and head north to Sedona to spend a day hiking, thinking, reflecting and discussing our future. A mutual friend contacted me that morning and let me know he was driving Farris from Flagstaff to the Phoenix airport, and could I meet with them?

So it was that Tracy and I found ourselves sitting in a Starbucks in Camp Verde, reflecting on our political experiences (Farris had been the Virginia GOP's nominee for Lt. Governor in 1993, also losing in the general election) and talking about the future.

Farris suggested I had a unique gifting and recommended I consider leading a Christian university—not knowing I would be asked to do exactly that nearly four years later. He spoke about building a network of high-academic Christian universities—a modern-day Ivy League—to prepare and train Christian leaders. On that day in November of 2006, he definitely planted a seed, although I had no idea how God would open that door and shove me through it years later.

Then, not long after becoming President of Arizona Christian University, I had opportunity to meet and spend time with inspirational Sen. Bill Armstrong, who served as President of Colorado Christian University in the Denver suburb of Lakewood from 2006 until his death in 2016.

I was familiar with President Armstrong initially due to his political career as a successful three-term U.S. Congressman and two-term U.S. Senator from Colorado during the Reagan years. He was that rare evangelical Christian politician, someone who returned from nearly two decades in our nation's Capitol with an even stronger Christian witness and a greater reputation for integrity and commitment to

INTRODUCTION

principle than when he left.

Then I heard from my oldest son, who attended and ultimately graduated from Colorado Christian University, about the incredibly positive changes that occurred at CCU when President Armstrong took office.

When I met with President Armstrong, he told me the most important element in CCU's resurgence—and the key to any Christian university's ability to stay on mission—was the adoption of what CCU referred to as "Strategic Objectives." These guiding principles provided a common purpose and a rallying point for the community, and a clear distinctive that separated CCU from most other colleges, even colleges with a historic Christian purpose. President Armstrong made the adoption of these objectives a condition of his employment at CCU.

After I shared my vision for a university that would equip and educate students to transform culture with biblical truth by preparing them to be leaders in the body of Christ in a wide range of disciplines and areas of influence, President Armstrong urged me to bring a similar set of principles to the Board of Trustees at Arizona Christian University. In 2012, that is what we did.

ACU's Core Commitments—with permission modeled on CCU's Strategic Objectives—were adopted after discussion and refinement by ACU's Trustees as the conservative, biblical guiding principles for our institution. They have been woven into our planning, our conversation, our accountability measures, our discussions with potential staff and faculty hires, and in the fall of 2014 became an important part of our new liberal arts curriculum—what we are referring to as "The CORE: Christian Liberal Arts for Cultural Transformation."

I know it can be confusing so let me try to clarify. Our curriculum as a University is based on our principles. Our principles are established by the Core Commitments—that's the one-page statement of principles adopted by our Board of Trustees in 2012 and explained in more detail by this book. Those principles led to the establishment in 2014 of our liberal arts curriculum—which is called "The CORE: Christian Liberal Arts for Cultural Transformation"—a series of courses taken by all ACU students that strategically integrates study of the humanities with the Bible.

This book is designed to clearly articulate and amplify the Core Commitments of ACU for students, staff, alumni and supporters of the University.

We at Arizona Christian University owe a debt of gratitude to President Armstrong for his inspirational leadership in the body of Christ and for his amazing generosity to ACU in sharing his ideas about higher education and the need for a set of conservative, biblical guiding principles for Christian universities.

President Armstrong died after a long battle with cancer on July 5, 2016. My last time to be with him and learn from him was in a Denver hospital over Memorial Day weekend in 2016, a few weeks before he passed into the presence of his Savior. President Armstrong was an incredible friend and mentor to me, even encouraging me to write this book and providing an endorsement for its first edition. I miss his booming radio voice, childlike enthusiasm for the gospel and his constant emphasis on "Jesus, Jesus, Jesus!" We need more leaders like Bill Armstrong, and more universities like Colorado Christian University.

The sense that something has gone deeply wrong with our country and our world is no longer confined to a handful of skeptics and pessimists. Apocalyptic films and sensational news headlines have been everywhere for the last decade. Economic uncertainty, international wars and civic unrest dominated news reports in recent years, leading to a widespread unease and fearfulness about the future.

And then 2020 happened.

All of the existing unease accelerated with the arrival of a global pandemic and subsequent lockdown, leading to vast and widespread job losses and economic uncertainty. The pandemic response, combined with increased political polarization and unsettling civic

INTRODUCTION

unrest, created a level of volatility unseen in more than a half-century. Civic unrest began with legitimate grievance and peaceful protests against ongoing incidents of racial injustice, but was quickly sidetracked by some activists into looting and property destruction as part of a broader and sometimes violent assault on law enforcement and the foundations of Western civilization and the United States.

Decades of secularization in our culture—due to the steady removal of a biblical worldview from every area of cultural influence, especially popular entertainment and our entire educational system—left Americans largely defenseless against these rapid and frightening developments. With no relationship with God to turn to provide historical context, comfort and peace, many Americans retreated into fear, anxiety, panic and depression. Suicide, drug overdose, alcoholism, domestic abuse—all of these increased and are warning signs of a decaying culture with no answers to the trials of life.

For Christ followers in America, it has felt like we have been on a long losing streak, helplessly watching this steady erosion of biblical truth's influence in our culture. So many responses to the decay and decline of our culture have seemed defensive in nature, trying to just hang on, to hold the line against further decline.

It is time for followers of Jesus to go back on offense, to go into all the world, and to be courageously Christian in a hostile culture. We need to build institutions of Christian influence that will last for generations, producing dedicated Christ followers who can bring the healing and hope of the gospel into every area of influence in our culture. In the same way that forces of secularization strategically gained influence in our culture over decades, we need to "play the long game" and build universities that reclaim education based on biblical truth to bring glory to God.

At ACU, we hope to inspire tomorrow's leaders to stand boldly for the things of God, and to bring biblical values and their faith in Christ into the center of culture as their generation moves into positions of influence in society.

ACU has specifically identified in its Core Commitments that there are several key areas of cultural influence and has sought to develop degree programs that will launch students into those vocations. Part of inspiring leaders is presenting examples of those who have been bold about their Christian faith while serving in positions of great influence—whether that influence vocationally is in the area of government, ministry, the family, business, education, media or entertainment.

ACU President Len Munsil thanks President George W. Bush after his speech March 16, 2011, at ACU's 50th anniversary celebration. (Photo by Timon G. Harper.)

In 2011 Arizona Christian University began a new tradition of recognizing and honoring such Christian leaders by presenting the Daniel Award for Courageous Public Faith. The first award went to former President George W. Bush for his open reliance on God and biblical principles through a challenging war-time presidency. Whether you agreed with his decisions or not, he was always clear that he sought to ground his decision-making in a biblical worldview and prayed for guidance as he dealt with each new challenge. President Bush urged nearly 1,300 attendees at the Daniel Award event to support the "good work" of ACU in preparing leaders for tomorrow. President Bush represented the "government" sphere of influence, reflected at ACU in our Political Science degree and pre-law emphasis.

INTRODUCTION

The Daniel Award recipient in 2012 was the Reverend Franklin Graham, president and CEO of both the Billy Graham Evangelistic Association and Samaritan's Purse. In speaking to supporters of ACU, Rev. Graham described Christian colleges and universities as "the last wall of defense against the rise of secularism" in America and the world.[12] Rev. Graham, through his work as an evangelist and his nonprofit relief work through Samaritan's Purse, represented the "church" or vocational ministry sphere of influence, reflected at ACU through our Biblical Studies and Christian Ministries degrees.

Rev. Franklin Graham speaks after receiving the 2012 Daniel Award from ACU.

Grammy Award–winning musician Michael W. Smith received our third Daniel Award in 2013 and performed a concert for an ACU audience.

Michael W. Smith performs after receiving the ACU 2013 Daniel Award.

Smith represented the "arts and entertainment" sphere of influence, though he achieved crossover fame in the secular recording industry, he remained faithful to producing worship through albums that glorified Christ. That sphere of influence is represented at ACU through our Music and Music Education degrees, and our praise and worship emphasis.

In 2015 the founders of Hobby Lobby, David and Barbara Green, came to ACU and addressed students at chapel and supporters at a dinner event, where we presented them with our fourth Daniel Award for Courageous Public Faith. The Greens were honored for the way they have conducted themselves as business owners through their commitment to sharing the gospel with and caring for their employees, along with their willingness to stand against an unjust government decree in order to defend innocent human life, all the way to the U.S. Supreme Court. The Greens represent the "marketplace" sphere of influence, reflected at ACU through our degree in Business Administration.

David and Barbara Green receive the 2015 Daniel Award from ACU Trustee Don King and his wife Mary King.

And in 2016, we celebrated a career dedicated to helping families by presenting the fifth Daniel Award for Courageous Public Faith to Dr. James Dobson, a psychologist who founded Focus on the Family and wrote multiple bestsellers about marriage and parenting. Generations of parents and families have been blessed by his wisdom and godly counsel that helped them build healthy families and marriages. Dr. Dobson represents the "family" sphere of influence, reflected at ACU through our degrees in Behavioral Health and Psychology, directed to using biblical counseling to restore marriages and strengthen family relationships.

Dr. James Dobson speaks after being presented with the 2016 Daniel Award from ACU.

As all of these leaders who have come to ACU have made clear, the need for a Christian university like Arizona Christian University that is committed to conservative, biblical principles has never been greater.

And as the President of ACU since 2010, I have watched the God of the universe move mountains—working through His people—to provide miracle after miracle of provision and opportunity for Arizona Christian University. I have watched miracles of transformation and redemption in hundreds of students who leave on a different, God-ordained trajectory after their time in ACU's authentic Christian community. I speak from experience when I say—God is in this! Without Him, we can do nothing. With Him, we can do anything.

ACU is here for such a time as this. Rather than play defense against an increasingly hostile culture, we must inspire winsome, persuasive, compassionate Christians who can move into centers of influence in our culture and lead their generation and future generations toward the hope and transformative change offered through a relationship with Jesus.

Only such an awakening will succeed in "transforming culture with truth."

Chapter Notes

1. Philip W. Eaton, *Engaging the Culture, Changing the World: The Christian University in a Post-Christian World*. (Downers Grove, IL: IVP Academic, 2011), 127.
2. Abraham Lincoln, Proclamation Appointing a National Fast-Day (1863), *The Papers and Writings of Abraham Lincoln*, Volume Six. Ed. Arthur Brooks Lapsley, The Project Gutenberg EBook, accessed August 20, 2014, http://www.gutenberg.org/files/2658/2658-h/2658-h.htm.
3. Mayflower Compact, 1620. Bruce Frohnen, *The American Republic: Primary Sources*, ed. Bruce Frohnen (Indianapolis: Liberty Fund, 2002). 10/1/2020. https://oll.libertyfund.org/titles/669#lf0082_head_022.
4. John Winthrop, "A Modell of Christian Charity," 1630. Collections of the Massachusetts Historical Society (Boston, 1838), 3rd series 7:31-48), 27. 10/1/2020. https://history.hanover.edu/texts/winthmod.html [Language modernized by author].
5. Barack Obama, "University of Massachusetts at Boston Commencement Address," June 2, 2006. 10/1/2020. http://obamaspeeches.com/074-University-of-Massachusetts-at-Boston-Commencement-Address-Obama-Speech.htm.
6. Eaton, 2011.
7. John Harvard, 1636. Tim LaHaye, *Faith of Our Founding Fathers* (Brentwood, TN: Wolgemuth & Hyatt Publishers, Inc., 1987), 32, quoted in William J. Federer, *America's God and Country: Encyclopedia of Quotations* (Amerisearch, Inc.: St. Louis, MO, 1999), 280.
8. "Rules and Precepts," (1636), Harvard University, *Old South Leaflets*, in *Sourcebook and Biographical Guide for American Church History*, Peter G. Mode, ed. (Menasha, WI: George Banta Publishing Co., 1921), 74-75, quoted in William J. Federer, *America's God and Country: Encyclopedia of Quotations* (Amerisearch, Inc.: St. Louis, MO, 1999), 280-281.
9. Harvard University, 1636, "Our Christian Heritage," *Letter from Plymouth Rock* (Marlborough, NH: The Plymouth Rock Foundation), 2, quoted in

INTRODUCTION

    William J. Federer, *America's God and Country: Encyclopedia of Quotations* (Amerisearch, Inc.: St. Louis, MO, 1999), 282.
10 "Rules and Precepts," 281.
11 Ibid.
12 Noah Webster, "Our Christian Heritage," *Letter from Plymouth Rock* (Marlborough, NH: The Plymouth Rock Foundation), 5, quoted in William J. Federer, *America's God and Country: Encyclopedia of Quotations* (Amerisearch, Inc.: St. Louis, MO, 1999), 676.
13 Franklin Graham, 2012. Speech, Daniel Award Banquet, Arizona Christian University, Phoenix, AZ, April 23, 2012.

Arizona Christian University Core Commitments

Arizona Christian University shall:

- Before all else, be committed to Jesus Christ – accomplishing His will and advancing His kingdom on earth as in heaven.
- Teach students to read, understand and trust the Bible, grounding them firmly in the truth through a biblical worldview.
- Be devoted to evangelism and to prayer without ceasing.
- Be committed to loving God with all our heart and soul, mind and strength, by pursuing excellence in spiritual formation, academics, athletics and extracurricular activities, doing all for the glory of God.
- Teach students to think critically, speak and write clearly and effectively, use technology effectively, develop interpersonal skills, and pursue personal and professional ethics through biblical literacy and integration.
- Provide opportunities for students to serve locally and globally, and promote a culture of lifelong commitment to servant-leadership.
- Influence, engage and transform the culture with truth by promoting the biblically informed values that are foundational to Western civilization, including:
    1. the centrality of family
    2. traditional sexual morality and lifelong marriage between one man and one woman
    3. the sanctity of human life
    4. compassion for the poor
    5. a biblical understanding of human nature
    6. an understanding of God's purposes for limited government
    7. personal, economic and religious freedom
    8. free markets, capitalism, and property rights
    9. natural law, the original meaning of the Constitution and judicial restraint
    10. international human rights and the advancement of freedom throughout the world.
- Prepare students to be leaders of influence in their community, state, nation and world – through the church, the family, business, government, education, health care, media, the arts and every area of society.
- Be a leading conservative Christian liberal arts university.

ONE

~

Arizona Christian University shall:
Before all else, be committed to Jesus Christ—accomplishing His will and advancing His kingdom on earth as in heaven.[1]

I am not a theologian. I'm not interested in getting into a debate on the end times and whether the return of Christ is imminent.

It's not that I don't care. I care deeply. Scripture teaches us that the Lord will return in power and glory, and when He does it will be a great day. If it happens during my lifetime on earth, then on that day I won't have to check off any more items on my to-do list, my back won't hurt anymore, and I won't have to pay any more bills or take out the garbage anymore. Hallelujah!

I have my opinions like every other Christian, maybe better-informed opinions than some, not nearly as informed as others. But my study of Scripture and history leads me to two conclusions of which I am completely confident:

1) Just about every generation of Christ followers since Jesus walked the earth believed they were living in the end times. So far, they've all been wrong, and yet they all had what we have—faith, access to Scripture, and varying levels of spiritual discernment. There are those today who think every drop in the stock market, every skirmish in the Middle East, every global disaster or pandemic is a certain sign of the Apocalypse. Might they be wrong—like every previous generation of Christians?

2) Jesus was clear that no one but God the Father would

know exactly the day or the hour of His return (Matthew 24:36). For me, that's enough. From my perspective, we don't need to spend a ton of time thinking about it. We know how things end, and for those who have trusted Christ for their salvation, it is very good. Heaven! No pain, no tears, lots of celebrating. But what about here and now? We are told to be on the alert and to live expectantly, not to sit around waiting to be rescued. We have things to do. In fact, once we have committed our lives to Jesus, our time and our very lives are not our own.

I Surrender All—*Before all else, be committed to Jesus Christ…*

But whatever gain I had, I counted as loss for the sake of Christ. Indeed, I count everything as loss because of the surpassing worth of knowing Christ Jesus my Lord. For his sake I have suffered the loss of all things and count them as rubbish, in order that I might gain Christ (Philippians 3:7–8).

I like leisure. I like entertainment. I enjoy going to movies and watching movies on TV. I like to read escapist fiction, usually action books involving men who dispense justice in some form, mainly to criminals or terrorists. I like to watch sports on television and in person.

Here are some interesting realities.

In my entire childhood, we went out to the movies maybe a dozen times or less. Movies on TV were rare and usually ran late at night or on weekend mornings. There were no recently released movies available. If you didn't see a movie in a theater, it would be years before you could see it on television, if ever. There were a grand total of six TV stations to watch in Phoenix, Arizona, one of the largest metro areas in America. At midnight these stations would sign off and the picture

CHAPTER ONE

would go to static overnight.

The genre of fiction I read now barely existed back then.

You could listen to music only on a handful of popular radio stations. If you found an artist you liked, you would head to the record store to buy an album and then play it on your home stereo. Your musical choices were largely limited to what was popular enough to hear on the radio.

When I was a boy, most sporting events that were televised occurred on weekends. My hometown basketball team, the Phoenix Suns, played 81 games, and only 13 were on television. Arizona didn't have professional football or baseball, and there was typically only one nationally televised baseball "game of the week" to watch, often on tape delay. During football season, it seemed like the whole world stopped to watch Monday Night Football.

Today by contrast, entertainment choices are omnipresent. There are a dozen new movies out in theaters every week of the year. Recent movies can be rented at any drugstore or grocery store for a dollar, or more likely, streamed online, along with a library of older films. Hundreds of entire television series are available for purchase, and "binge watching" entire seasons of TV shows is the norm.

Today there are dozens of prominent authors turning out at least one book per year each in the escapist genres I enjoy most.

Through streaming, music fans can explore every genre of music available and listen to any song by any artist at any time.

And now sports fans can watch live sporting events just about every waking hour, plus great interviews and sports news coverage 24/7. Seasons have been extended and often overlap, more and more athletic teams and individual competitions have been created for a variety of sports—and yet there seems to be no risk of saturation or slowing.

The truth is, in today's world, we could entertain ourselves all the time, every waking moment, from childhood until death, and never run out of music, movies, TV shows and sports events to watch. When we leave home we take our entertainment with us on our phones and tablets. And the things we are watching and listening to are really entertaining! I could probably fill my entire schedule each year just reading the kind of books I like to read for semi-mindless entertainment. I could certainly watch enough entertaining TV shows, movies or athletic contests to avoid doing much of anything else in my life.

Oh, and also—social media! Another assault on the meaningful use of our limited time on earth. Between Twitter, Instagram, Tik Tok, Snapchat, Facebook—and whatever new social media site emerges in the days ahead—we have to actually consciously force ourselves to emerge from this all-encompassing virtual world into real life.

The biggest difference from my childhood is there are no times of pausing, in the year, the season, the week, the day, the hour, no breaks from the omnipresent reality of entertainment—music, TV, movies, sports. There are no overnights with television off the air, no moments without access to music, no escape from social media notifications. No time to be alone with your thoughts—and with your God. Unless we make it.

No matter how you spend your leisure time, the reality is that every genre of entertainment and leisure activity that people enjoy has expanded and can be consumed constantly in our 24/7 world.

When I arrived at Arizona Christian University in the fall of 2010, the school had an aging infrastructure and limited Internet connectivity maintained by a one-person IT department. "You better hope he doesn't get hit by a truck," said my Dad, a retired Motorola software manager who volunteered his time a few days a week to help out. "You'd have to shut down the school."

Over the next few years, we added multiple new staff positions and poured massive resources into IT and Internet upgrades. And yet, to my great frustration, no matter how many upgrades we made, it seemed like every year we had connectivity issues. After an outage that led to my third "This can never happen again!" meeting with senior executives at the school, I asked why solutions were so elusive.

CHAPTER ONE

"Simple," I was told. "In the last few years, the average student has gone from zero or one wireless device to three or four. They're always online, and there are lots of movies and TV shows being streamed at any time of the day or night. As soon as we upgrade capacity and bandwidth, it's overwhelmed by increased usage."

It takes incredible discipline, particularly for young people raised in a media- and entertainment-focused culture, to turn away from all of that, even for a time, to focus on anything else. Tiny little life issues like, for example, our relationship with God. Relationships with family and friends. Classwork. Jobs. Exercise. All suffer. At least in America, and much of the West, our pursuit of a significant, healthy and balanced life has been diminished by our unlimited access to media, entertainment and leisure activities.

Leisure, entertainment, the arts and even social media can add emotional connection, depth and balance to the quality of our lives. But not if we are so busy entertaining ourselves or spending so much time in the virtual world that we forget to live life, or neglect to pursue God's plan and purpose for our life.

Contrast the distractions available to young people today with the life of David during his youth. The shepherd's life involved quite a bit of downtime. It got dark early and no streetlights came on. All that darkness and downtime allowed David seasons of deep contemplation of his Creator, and led to some of the most beautiful and inspired poetic writing in world history:

> When I consider your heavens, the work of your fingers,
> The moon and the stars, which You have ordained;
> What is man that you take thought of him,
> And the son of man that You care for him? (Psalm 8:3–4)

With all of life's distractions in the early 21st Century, we have to choose to spend time with God and learn His ways. We have to choose prayer, meditation on the things of God, Scripture reading, fellowship, and worship over the pull of the latest social media notification or binge-worthy TV series. We have to choose our commitment to Jesus Christ, "before all else"—or the "all else" will become our life.

As a kid playing baseball, whenever one of us would dive for a ground ball, someone would yell, "Way to sacrifice your body!" As Christ followers, that's actually what we are called to do. Paul wrote, "I appeal to you therefore, brothers, by the mercies of God, to present your bodies as a living sacrifice, holy and acceptable to God, which is your spiritual worship" (Romans 12:1).

Jesus asked for even more. "Then Jesus told his disciples, 'If anyone would come after me, let him deny himself and take up his cross and follow me. For whoever would save his life will lose it, but whoever loses his life for my sake will find it. For what will it profit a man if he gains the whole world and forfeits his soul?" (Matthew 16:24–26).

As Christ followers, our lives, our bodies, our time, no longer belong to us. They belong to the God who created us.

The Will of God—...*accomplishing His will*...

So, God created us and redeemed us through Jesus. Now what? Or, as theologian Francis Schaeffer asked in the title of his groundbreaking 1976 book, *How Should We Then Live?*

The Bible is full of instruction on how we should relate to God and to each other. Instruction is always given for our good, not to punish us or restrict us. The Old Testament describes the creation of the world and of the first man and woman. Immediately after creating Adam and Eve, God provided our first instructions: "God blessed them; and God said to them, 'Be fruitful and multiply, and fill the earth, and subdue it; and rule over the fish of the sea and over the birds of the sky and over every living thing that moves on the earth'" (Genesis 1:28).

This is often referred to as the "cultural mandate." In essence, God plants the first humans in a garden, and tells them (us) to create families and fill the earth by participating in activities of creation

CHAPTER ONE

and culture and work that lead to human flourishing and dominion. Despite our rebellion against God during the fall, this mandate is never revoked. Richard J. Mouw, former president and professor of philosophy at Fuller Theological Seminary, explains God's plan in his book, *Abraham Kuyper: A Short and Personal Introduction:*

> Human rebellion made a mess of what God originally intended for the creation. But...God looked down upon this rebellious humanity and decided to start something new. He decided to choose a specific people—the ethnic Israelites, Abraham's descendants—to be special recipients of his sovereign grace. He called them to organize their lives so as to show the rest of the world what it is like to live in obedience to the will of the Creator in all dimensions of human life. He gave them instructions not only about how to worship, but also about farming, family life, politics, economics, the fashioning of beautiful things, their relationships with other tribes and nations—in short, God chose Israel as a means of putting on display some of his original intentions for cultural processes and products. Once again there would be people on the earth who would direct their lives toward his glory, "filling the earth" and "having dominion" in ways that pleased the Creator.
>
> The initiative that God took with ancient Israel, however, was the first stage of something much more significant that God would eventually bring about. There came a time when the eternal God appeared in the flesh, as Jesus of Nazareth, to guarantee the success of the initiative begun in more ancient times.[2]

With man's rejection of God's plan in the garden, God ultimately provides Jesus to bridge the gap between man and God that was created by our sin. Jesus is the redeemer, but He is also the restorer of all that was lost in our understanding of our role and our participation in

God's created order. He is the one in whom "all things hold together" (Colossians 1:17).

As Mouw puts it: "That the redemption accomplished by Christ heals what was wounded by the Fall is certainly true in the redeeming of individuals.... But redemption reaches far beyond individuals."[3] Ultimately, "our salvation as individuals includes the obligation to align ourselves with God's desire that his will is to be acknowledged and glorified in all areas of life. Our discipleship includes cultural obedience."[4]

When Jesus ascends to the Father, He leaves us with the Great Commission: "Go therefore and make disciples of all nations, baptizing them in the name of the Father and of the Son and the Holy Spirit, teaching them to observe all that I have commanded you. And behold, I am with you always to the end of the age" (Matthew 28:19–20).

Again, we have clear instructions. Make disciples throughout the world, baptizing them and ultimately teaching them everything Jesus taught us. That is how we can accomplish His will.

The Kingdom of God—*...advancing his kingdom on earth as in heaven.*

Maybe like me you have heard variations of this message at times from Christians or from your church: "I don't care at all about [politics, the economy, culture, etc.]. We already know the world is just going to keep going downhill until God destroys it all."

What a depressing, pessimistic, wrong-headed, and flawed message. If I believed that, I'm not sure why I would keep showing up every day...for anything.

The issue here isn't even about how the end comes or what it looks like. The issue is whether we should *care*. In a nutshell, the question is whether we should try to make the world a better place, or just let it fall apart.

To conclude that we should just let the world fall apart would fly

CHAPTER ONE

in the face of so many scriptural passages that provide instruction on how we should live, how we relate to each other, how we should love and serve one another, and how we are to engage as "salt and light" in a fallen world.

And as we shall see, spiritual decline is not inevitable. Not in our own lives and not in the lives of cultures and nations. Revivals and awakenings do occur, and they are genuine game-changers.

But perhaps the most obvious refutation of that pessimistic mindset comes from the mouth of Jesus himself, when he taught us to pray: "Thy Kingdom come, thy will be done, on earth as it is in heaven" (Matthew 6:10). Jesus taught us to pray that the will of God would be done on earth as it is in heaven. It's hard to reconcile that prayer with the notion that we should let the world fall apart. Instead, it should be seen for what it is—a call to engagement in the world, using the principles of God that Jesus taught us.

What would such a world look like? We have seen glimpses on this earth of the peace, prosperity, safety, and joy we imagine in heaven from those cultures and communities most heavily influenced by biblical Christianity. It will never be perfect—not this side of heaven, due to man's sinful nature. But the prayer of Jesus that we would pursue God's will on earth as in heaven has to mean something. To me, it means that as Christians, we should do our best to learn, teach and live out the principles of God in our own lives, and also in every area of the world we touch.

In fantasy writer Stephen Lawhead's series of fictional books about King Arthur, he describes what a community might look like that lived out the principles of Christianity. Lawhead, who writes generally from a biblical worldview, provides a beautiful, aspirational and inspirational vision of the kind of community I believe Jesus is asking us to pray for and to work toward. In reality, it is a picture of heaven, the Kingdom of God—the very Kingdom Jesus asks us to pray would come "on earth as in heaven":

There is a land, a land of shining goodness where each man

protects his brother's dignity as readily as his own, where war and want have ceased and all tribes live under the same law of love and honor. It is a land bright with truth, where a man's word is his pledge and falsehood is banished, where children sleep safe in their mother's arms and never know fear or pain. It is a land where kings extend their hands in justice rather than reach for the sword; where mercy, kindness, and compassion flow like deep water, and where men revere virtue, revere truth, revere beauty above comfort, pleasure or selfish gain. A land where peace reigns in the hearts of men. Where faith blazes like a beacon from every hill and love like a fire from every hearth; where the True God is worshipped and His ways acclaimed by all.[5]

That vision stirs my soul. I believe it is a vision of a nation, community and culture transformed by truth.

Chapter Notes

1. ACU Core Commitments, adopted by ACU Board of Trustees, Nov. 8, 2012. Available on page 27 of this text and at: https://www arizonachristian.edu/about/mission.
2. Richard J. Mouw, *Abraham Kuyper: A Short and Personal Introduction* (Grand Rapids, MI: Wm. B. Eerdmans Publishing Company, 2011), 11-12.
3. Ibid., 13.
4. Ibid., 15.
5. Stephen R. Lawhead, *Taliesin* (New York: HarperCollins, Inc. 1987), 443.

TWO

~

Arizona Christian University shall:
Teach students to read, understand and trust the Bible...

> All Scripture is breathed out by God and profitable for teaching, for reproof, for correction, and for training in righteousness, that the man of God may be complete, equipped for every good work.
>
> 2 TIMOTHY 3:16

In many ways Arizona Christian University is the spiritual heir of Ivy League institutions of higher learning, like Harvard, that began with a focus on the truth of Scripture. I've visited Harvard's campus and seen the famous statue of John Harvard, his right hand resting on an open Bible. Harvard's well-known motto of *Veritas*—Truth—has been shortened from its original motto of *Veritas pro Christo et ecclesia*, which means "Truth for Christ and his Church." The original motto can still be seen on several gates to Harvard Yard, as well as in Harvard's Memorial Hall and Sanders Theatre. In its first century as a college, more than half of Harvard graduates became full-time Christian pastors. Today, Harvard needs Christian missionaries, which is why I am thankful for a recent ACU graduate who went to Harvard Law School.

Arizona Christian University has a Harvard connection at its foundation. Our first president, Dr. Wallace Woods, attended Harvard for graduate school in addition to studying at Stanford and at Wheaton College. In the fall of 2010, when I was inaugurated as the sixth President of then–Southwestern College, Dr. Woods was in attendance and offered a public prayer of blessing at the outset of the ceremony. Dr. Woods lived in the West Valley, where he regularly attended his local Baptist church, which was pastored by a Southwestern College graduate. Shortly before his death in October of 2014, he visited campus and we had a chance to catch up regarding the new things happening at ACU. He told me he prayed for me and ACU every day.

Dr. Wallace Woods, ACU's first president, visits with President Munsil on campus in 2014.

More than a half-century ago, Dr. Woods, who served as President until 1975, wrote about the purpose of then–Southwestern College:

> We want to be current in our thinking and up-to-date in our methods. We want to be relevant to the changing needs of people. Nevertheless, there are foundations upon which we stand as a Bible college, and *we fix our anchor in the authority of the scriptures*. By God's grace we want to be flexible in the application of Biblical principles to the training of students for effective service in their respective careers and yet hold steadfastly to the Statement of Faith which has characterized the College since its founding.[1]

The founders of what was originally known as Southwestern Conservative Baptist Bible College, along with Dr. Woods, laid a solid

CHAPTER TWO

foundation in the "authority of the scriptures" and sought to prioritize the teaching of biblical truth in the broader context of a college education. Today, when we continue the university's original mission of teaching students to "read, understand, and trust the Bible," we keep faith with those thousands of men and women who not only prayed, but also sacrificed their time, talent and treasure to start this Bible college in the desert more than a half-century ago.

God's miraculous provision for Arizona Christian University started long before the college began, through the vision and generosity of a Christian nurse who moved to Arizona from Ohio. Miss Ida Clouse came to Arizona Territory before the turn of the 19th Century and worked at St. Joseph Hospital. She was granted 160 acres of land under the Homestead Act put into place by President Abraham Lincoln in 1862. When Miss Clouse died in 1946, she was penniless but land rich. Without heirs, she left the land in care of the pastor of Calvary Bible Church, where she had been active. Miss Clouse was known to be particularly supportive of ministry that was dedicated to preparing young people for Christian service. In her bequest, her only requirement was that the land would be used "for Christian purposes." Over decades, the land she left to the church was used for Christian camps, and ultimately much of it would be sold to provide for multiple Christian ministries, churches and missionary work. However, 35 acres of land was provided to the Conservative Baptist denomination for a Christian college— Southwestern College, which began in 1960 on that site.

By the time I became President of then-Southwestern College in 2010, all but 18 of the 35 acres had been sold off. After changing our name to ACU in 2011, the University quickly outgrew that campus. But by another miracle of God, ACU in 2018 was able to trade that land for a new, 68-acre campus in Glendale filled with nearly 500,000 square feet of academic buildings—the former home of the Thunderbird School of Global Management. In 2019, ACU began operations on this new campus and by 2020 surpassed 1,000 students for the first time.

All of this began with a Christian woman's incredible faith and her desire to make a difference for the Kingdom beyond her own lifetime. She had no children or grandchildren, and no money when she died. But because of her amazing faith and commitment to the Lord, ACU has been able to provide a Bible-based college education for 60 years for thousands of young people who want to serve God. Someday we will be able to meet her and celebrate her gift in person!

The story of Southwestern College/Arizona Christian University is filled with miracles of God's provision. I know some of them, but others are known only to God and to those who served or attended the college throughout its history. But I believe God has made provision for ACU again and again because from its beginning, it has been committed to teaching students "to read, understand and trust the Bible." Many things have changed since 1960, "but the word of our God stands forever" (Isaiah 40:8).

If you look at the pictures in old yearbooks from Southwestern College in the 1960s, you will see young male students in jackets and ties and female students in long dresses. As Dr. Woods saw even then, the school would need to be "relevant to the changing needs of people." Dress codes and other institutional rules (no dancing, no movies) have transitioned from what could be considered legalistic, to an emphasis on biblical standards of modesty and decorum.

When former NBA All-Star and Hall of Famer Paul Westphal, a strong evangelical Christian, was recruited to begin his coaching career at Southwestern College, in essence as a volunteer, he was interviewed on topics including smoking, drinking, dancing and movies.

Having lit a few victory cigars with legendary NBA Coach and General Manager Red Auerbach during his playing career with the Boston Celtics, Westphal nevertheless committed to not smoke any stogies while coaching at the college. But he couldn't help but think, "Didn't C.S. Lewis use a pipe? Could he have taught here?" When it came to alcohol and dancing, he was thinking, "Didn't Jesus turn water into wine? And didn't David lead the dancing after battlefield

CHAPTER TWO

victories?" But as he told me later, he wanted the job! So, he agreed to the rules, which applied to faculty and staff as well as students.

Today ACU maintains a strong commitment to biblical standards of conduct. And all students sign a community covenant. But the goal of Student Life leaders is not to "catch students" in violations of the covenant, but to help them navigate through an exciting but challenging time of life, moving from adolescence into adulthood, with mutual accountability. Love, grace and opportunities for redemption and renewal are frequently offered to students who fall short of behavioral standards, with biblical counsel and compassionate accountability.

Out of respect and appreciation for our heritage, and because of our roots as a Bible college, Arizona Christian University is the only accredited university in Arizona that requires a minor in Bible for every graduate of our institution—18 credit hours of Bible courses that provide a thorough grounding in the Word of God. Those Bible courses are above and beyond the biblical worldview that is integrated through all courses and academic disciplines.

While most Christian colleges today require only one or two faith-related courses, ACU graduates receive a lifelong blessing that will bear fruit for generations—a deep intellectual understanding of God's word in the context of human history. As it is written in Joshua 1:8:

> This Book of the Law shall not depart from your mouth, but you shall meditate on it day and night, so that you may be careful to do according to all that is written in it. For then you will make your way prosperous, and then you will have good success.

Now, with the new "CORE: Liberal Arts for Cultural Transformation" curriculum, our students will learn that the Bible is accurate, authentic and inerrant—not only a guide to live by but also a reliable account of world history. Blessings will flow from our students' study and meditation on God's word.

The landscape of higher education across America is littered with universities that have abandoned their commitment to biblical truth. Some still bear the name of Christ or claim to offer a Christian education, yet are often today staffed by administrators and faculty who seem committed to tearing down the authority of Scripture, mocking the Christian faith, and ridiculing the truth claims of Christianity.

Alliance Defending Freedom, a national legal ministry defending religious freedom, now has an entire portion of its ministry dedicated to providing legal support for Christian students, faculty and staff who are seeking to exercise their rights to study, pray and form Christian organizations on public university campuses.

Of the first 108 college and universities in America, 106 of them were created to teach the Bible in the context of higher education. Today, Christians on many campuses are fighting just for the right to exercise their faith without being punished by their universities.[2]

As a private Christian university, ACU has the ability and opportunity to boldly teach the Scriptures and weave biblical truth into every class, understanding that a firm foundation in truth is an asset no matter what discipline or career a student pursues.

...grounding them firmly in truth through a biblical worldview.

> Every word of God proves true; he is a shield to those who take refuge in Him.
>
> Proverbs 30:5

Some might ask, why all this emphasis on grounding students in truth, as it says in ACU's vision—to "transform culture with truth"? The answer is simple. As the Proverbs declare, "Every word of God proves true." Today the very concept of truth is under assault, particularly among young people. And yet the truths of Scripture and the gospel are exactly what we need to bring hope and purpose to our lives and reformation to our decaying culture.

Dr. George Barna is the nation's leading researcher on public opinion and trends in the Christian community. For decades he has

CHAPTER TWO

been chronicling the significant decline of biblical worldview thinking in our nation.

In 2019 we were thrilled to have Dr. Barna join Arizona Christian University as a member of our faculty and as Director of Research for the new Cultural Research Center at Arizona Christian University. The Cultural Research Center's mission is "to advance the Kingdom of God by conducting cultural and biblical worldview studies that will provide research and resources to inform and mobilize strategic engagement in cultural transformation."[3]

In its first year, CRC actively measured the biblical worldview of Americans through its *American Worldview Inventory 2020* survey research. A series of releases from the *AWVI 2020* have attracted national and international attention to ACU. CRC is providing Dr. Barna's research as data to the broader Christian community. As a result ACU is fast on its way to becoming known as the nation's pre-eminent biblical worldview university.

This data can help us understand what is necessary to re-engage the body of Christ with the important task of helping Christians to "think like Jesus" and live according to biblical truth.

At the same time, ACU is the first Christian university to actively test its success in building biblical worldview among its students. Beginning in the fall of 2020, all ACU students will anonymously take the *ACU Student Worldview Inventory*, a worldview test developed by Dr. Barna at the start of each year and again when they graduate. This will enable us to benchmark their progress in developing a biblical worldview during their time as students at ACU. The results of these surveys will enable ACU to make adjustments where necessary to our academic and spiritual life programs to improve outcomes for our students.

Results from the *American Worldview Inventory* have already demonstrated a continued decline in biblical worldview and our nation's understanding of truth.

In the very first report issued by Dr. Barna and CRC, the survey research showed that only half as many Americans have a biblical worldview compared to 25 years previously—6 percent compared to 12 percent a quarter-century ago.[4]

The latest research confirms that those trends continue downward by age, which makes the importance of training young Christians in biblical worldview at ACU even more vital. For those over age 50, only 9 percent have a biblical worldview. Only 5 percent of people in their 30s and 40s have a biblical worldview, while just 2 percent of 18- to 29-year-olds hold a biblical view of the world.[5]

Even in the body of Christ, there is much work to be done. Only 19 percent of born-again Christians hold a biblical worldview.[6] At the same time, only 43 percent of born-again Christians believe there is absolute truth.[7]

I remember in my first year of law school, during a philosophical argument related to the nature and definition of crime, one of the more outspoken members of our Criminal Law class declared boldly that "[w]e all know there is no absolute truth!" The professor quickly replied, "Are you absolutely sure?"

Despite the conundrum of those who are absolute in their belief that there are no absolutes, you would have to expect some confusion about absolutes among non-Christians in a culture so heavily influenced by moral relativism, and so unaware of the ways of God. After all, if you do not recognize the source of truth, it is much easier to deny its existence.

But for those who identify as born-again Christians, the numbers are shocking and disconcerting—nearly half (48 percent) of all born-again Christians agreed with this statement: "Identifying moral truth is up to each individual; there are no moral absolutes that apply to every person, all the time."[8]

For followers of Jesus Christ, this makes no sense. Jesus Himself not only spoke about truth, but also declared that He was the Truth! He said quite clearly "I am the way, and the truth, and the life; no one comes to the father but through me" (John 14:6).

CHAPTER TWO

How you can be a follower of Jesus Christ and reject his own words and declaration as it relates to truth is beyond me. But the result is obvious—rather than Christians gently leading the world back toward the truth, instead it appears from Dr. Barna's research that the world's rejection of truth is influencing Christian thinking away from the authority of God and His word.

The effect of our culture's rejection of God's truth is all around us—utter devastation.

If we reject the truth of who God is and who we are as His creation, then why would we care about the value and dignity of every human life? And so we see a culture of death developing in our society—not only the wholesale cultural embrace of our ability to control when and how God creates new life but also the self-granted authority to take innocent human life in the womb and to end life that no longer meets our definition of worth and productivity. Insensitivity to life is reflected now in our laws, even though our founding document declares that we are "endowed by our Creator with certain unalienable rights, that among these are life…".

At the same time, if we reject the truth that each human being is created in the image of God, then it becomes easy to justify racist thinking and attitudes, or violence by the strong against the weak and powerless, or mistreatment of the poor by the rich. So many of the divisions in our culture today flow from rejection of God's truths about the value and dignity of every human life.

There are enormous consequences for society resulting from our rejection of the truth.

Today we are busy rejecting the truth that God ordained the institution of marriage as a lifetime commitment between a man and a woman. And as we reject that truth, we see cohabitation and divorce become the norm for our society, and the Supreme Court has even redefined what constitutes a legal marriage to include same sex relationships. Yet we know that generations of young people will suffer as a result of our society's rejection of the truth Jesus gave us in Matthew

19:5: "For this reason a man will leave his father and mother and be joined to his wife, and the two will become one flesh." Not only those who enter into damaging sexual relationships outside of male-female marriage, but the children raised without the benefit of a married mother and father—one of the most important elements in determining whether a child will flourish.

More recently, we have begun to reject the foundational truth that "male and female He created them" (Genesis 1:27)—a basic biological, scientific fact that has now given way to the madness of politically correct gender revisionism and "transgender" activism.

Of course, the most significant consequence of our rejection of the concept of truth is eternal, not temporal. Whatever happens here on earth, we know that a person's rejection of the truth of Jesus Christ and His sacrifice leads to eternal separation from a loving God.

These are incredibly hard truths to speak in a culture that is offended by the mere assertion that truth exists. And yet, to ignore these truths or to be unwilling to speak them is to consign generations to lives of misery and unhappiness and to a future without hope. To ignore these truths—even in the face of widespread cultural opposition—is to fail to "love your neighbor as yourself."

In Romans 15:4, we read that "…whatever was written in former days was written for our instruction, that through endurance and the encouragement of the Scriptures we might have hope."

That's one of the reasons I'm so excited about what God is doing at Arizona Christian University. At ACU, the truth about God and His word is not only welcome—it is essential.

In order for truth to invade and influence our world, someone has to know it, and someone has to be the keeper and defender of the truth. Christian higher education at a Bible-believing and teaching university is one of the few remaining places in our culture, outside the church itself, where Christian truth can be taught and integrated within broader educational purposes in a way that transforms lives.

Education without a foundation in biblical truth is a scary proposition, yet that is exactly what most college students today are receiving. As Martin Luther wrote:

> I am afraid that the schools will prove the very gates of hell, unless they diligently labour in explaining the Holy Scriptures, and engraving them on the hearts of youth. I would advise no one to send his child where the Holy Scriptures are not supreme. Every institution in which men and women are not unceasingly occupied with the Word of God must be corrupt.[9]

Obviously, Luther felt strongly about centering all education around the authority of Scripture. And Scripture reminds us in Proverbs 1:7 that "The fear of the Lord is the beginning of knowledge."

Education without any moral guidance from Scripture can actually be quite damaging. During an ethics class in law school I recall pointing out that simply teaching the rules of professional responsibility or legal ethics, without providing any value judgments about truth, or right and wrong—any reference point for a true view of the world—would only have the effect of teaching future lawyers how to be dishonest while technically staying within the rules. Without a moral compass, skirting ethical rules without violating them becomes something of a game for educated people.

A biblical worldview is essentially a view of the world framed by biblical truth. That framework leads and guides the way we respond to the challenges and opportunities of life, and provides a guide and a reference point for every human interaction. As Dr. Barna has written:

> [W]hile most people never think about their worldview on a conscious level, everyone has one. Our moment-to-moment decisions are shaped by the worldview that we have adopted, adapted and applied over the course of time…
>
> Whenever we make a decision, we unconsciously run it through a mental and emotional filter that allows us to make choices consistent with what we believe to be true, signifi-

cant and appropriate. That filter is the result of how we have organized information to make sense of the world in which we live....

A *biblical worldview* is a means of experiencing, interpreting and responding to reality in light of biblical perspective. This view provides a personal understanding of every idea, opportunity and experience based on identification and application of relevant biblical principles so that each choice we make may be consistent with God's principles and commands. At the risk of seeming simplistic, it is asking the question, "what would Jesus do if He were in my shoes right now?" and applying the answer without compromising because of how we anticipate the world reacting.[10]

The departure from biblical truth in our culture is profound and overwhelming. Dr. Barna's research reveals that fewer than one in five of those who profess to be Christians are thinking through issues and living their life consistently with their beliefs.

On the plus side—what an incredible opportunity for this generation of Christ followers! Because 98-plus percent of young adults are making day-to-day decisions without any ethical grounding based on God's truth, the results will be catastrophic. ACU students, with a foundation in biblical wisdom combined with compassion for their friends and peers, will have incredible opportunities to minister hope and healing to their generation.

ACU is strategically integrating biblical truth and faith in Christ in every subject matter taught, mentoring in biblical truth through every extracurricular and athletic event, along with service and spiritual formation requirements, and then measuring the results to improve outcomes. By helping our students push back against the lies of our culture and embrace a biblical worldview, we believe they can integrate the ethics and faith of Christ into their every decision and activity. By doing so, and by mentoring and guiding others in their generation, they will have a profound and transformational effect on

CHAPTER TWO

the world.

Jesus, the source and personification of truth, prayed that we would understand and embrace truth. The night before he was crucified, Jesus prayed with his disciples, as it is recorded in John, Chapter 17, beginning at Verse 14:

> I have given them Your word; and the world has hated them, because they are not of the world, even as I am not of the world. I do not ask You to take them out of the world, but to keep them from the evil one. They are not of the world, even as I am not of the world. *Sanctify them in the truth; Your word is truth.* As You sent Me into the world, I also have sent them into the world (emphasis added).

These verses speak to us today. We have God's word. And if we are preaching the word of God in a way that wins the favor of the world, then maybe we aren't preaching the whole truth. Jesus tells us the world will hate us because we are not of this world.

In many foreign countries we are witnessing a renewal of the persecution of Christians, who are being martyred for refusing to renounce their faith in Christ. In America hostility to Christianity and biblical truth is dramatically on the increase. Quite simply, it takes more courage today to stand for Christ in our culture than it did even a generation ago. As we equip students at ACU, one of our tag lines is "Courageously Christian"—providing a glimpse of what will be required of our students and all of us in the days ahead.

Jesus prays for our protection, but he does *not* pray that we be taken out of the world, no matter how hostile it becomes. Instead, we realize we are called to be salt and light, and to bring light to the dark places of this world. So, Jesus sends us into the world, armed with the truth of His word.

Our vision at Arizona Christian University is to see transformation, first in our own lives as we are sanctified in truth as our understanding is formed through the study of Scripture, and then to the culture and the world around us. We know that truth transforms, and that God's word and His truth have power all their own and will never return without any effect (Isaiah 55:11).

At ACU we have an important purpose and role to play in standing for God's truth, in equipping Christian leaders to know the source of truth, and helping to give them the courage to speak the truth in love to their generation.

On many mornings I will read some short, simple devotionals written by the late Hal M. Helms, called *Echoes of Eternity: Listening to the Father*. His devotionals are designed around his quiet time in the Bible; he would simply journal what he sensed God was speaking to him. One morning as I contemplated this commitment of ACU to teaching biblical truth, I read this devotional:

> Stand in truth. Seek the truth and pursue it. Truth often cuts, sometimes wounds, but only to heal. Do not fear the truth. Stand in it boldly. Speak it courageously, even when it threatens a false peace. Know that I, the Lord, am the God of truth. Know that I, the Son of God, am the truth embodied in a human life. Respect the truth, nay, reverence and honor it—for the truth brings life.[11]

Chapter Notes

1. Wallace Woods, Ph.D., on purpose of Southwestern College, 1975, historical documents, Arizona Christian University Library.
2. "Letter from Plymouth Rock," The Plymouth Rock Foundation, http://fpparchive.org/wp-content/uploads/2014/01/Letter-from-Plymouth-Rock_noauthor_nodate_The-Plymouth-Rock-Foundation.pdf, 2.
3. Cultural Research Center at Arizona Christian University, https://www.arizonachristian.edu/culturalresearchcenter/.
4. George Barna, "CRC Survey Shows Dangerously Low Percentage of Americans Hold Biblical Worldview," *American Worldview Inventory 2020* Release #1: "Worldviews in America" (March 24, 2020), 1. https://www.arizonachristian.edu/wp-content/uploads/2020/04/CRC-AWVI-2020-

CHAPTER TWO

Release_01-Worldview-in-America.pdf.
5   Barna, "Millennials Have Radically Different Beliefs about Respect, Faith, and America," *American Worldview Inventory 2020* Release #11: Worldview in the Millennial Generation" (September 22, 2020), 1. https://www.arizonachristian.edu/wp-content/uploads/2020/10/CRC_AWVI2020_Release10_Digital_03_20200922.pdf.
6   Barna, "Is the Bible True? CRC Survey Shows America's Distrust of the Bible Undermines Its Worldview," *American Worldview Inventory 2020* Release #2: Faith and Worldview (April 7, 2020), 2. https://www.arizonachristian.edu/wp-content/uploads/2020/04/CRC-AWVI-2020-Release-02_Faith-and-Worldview-1.pdf.
7   Barna, "Survey Finds Americans See Many Sources of Truth—and Reject Moral Absolutes," *American Worldview Inventory 2020* Release #5: Perceptions of Truth (May 19, 2020), 1. https://www.arizonachristian.edu/wp-content/uploads/2020/05/AWVI-2020-Release-05-Perceptions-of-Truth.pdf.
8   Ibid., 2.
9   Martin Luther, cited in William H. Jeynes and David Robinson, "Character Education in Higher Education: A Historical Analysis and Contemporary Change, Part I," *Christian Higher Education* 9, no. 4 (2010), 297.
10 Barna, *Think Like Jesus: Make the Right Decision Every Time* (Brentwood, TN: Integrity Publishers, 2003), 21–22.
11 Hal M. Helms, *Echoes of Eternity: Listening to the Father*, vol. 1 (Orleans, MA: Paraclete Press, Inc., 1996).

THREE

Arizona Christian University shall:
Be devoted to evangelism and to prayer without ceasing.

Because ACU is an accredited university first and foremost, with an educational purpose, some might wonder whether an emphasis on evangelism and prayer is appropriate. But at Arizona Christian University, this focus on evangelism and prayer is a reminder that, although the product for students is a degree in a particular discipline, we are Christians first and everything else second. The University was founded and continues to exist in order to glorify God and to prepare followers of Jesus to "walk worthy" of our calling—in this case, through our experience in an academic community (Ephesians 4:1).

Being part of a community of Christians in a university setting provides unique opportunities to participate and grow in these important disciplines of the faith.

Be devoted to evangelism...

At various points in our Christian walk, we hear about "lifestyle" evangelism, "relational" evangelism, "friendship" evangelism, "prayer" evangelism, or even "confrontational" evangelism and "Internet" evangelism.

But evangelism is not a technique or a program or a methodology. It's not a formula that will work every time if we just follow it precisely. Evangelism flows out of the heartbeat of who we are as followers of Jesus—people saved and redeemed and reconciled to God not through any effort or good works on our part, but through God's gift of His son Jesus.

Jesus is fully God and yet fully man—a real person who walked the earth more than 2,000 years ago, who claimed to be the Son of God and proved it through His words, miracles, and ultimately His death, burial, and resurrection. These are historical events with thousands of witnesses.

God sent Jesus to earth not to condemn us but to save us (John 3:17, 12:47). Our rebellion and sin against God separates us from Him and ultimately from the hope of heaven. By embracing the sacrifice of a sinless Jesus and inviting Him to live within us, when God looks at our hearts He no longer sees our sin but our faith in His perfect Son, who took the penalty for our sin. Thus perfected by our faith in Christ, we are reconciled to God! The gateway to heaven is opened.

This is the gospel, the "good news." And it's all true!

Having received this good news, and knowing God's love for people and His desire that they "not perish but come to repentance" (2 Peter 3:9), we long as Christians to share this good news with those around us. Evangelism should be the natural result of our relationship with Christ and our desire to "love one another" as He has loved us.

After the resurrection of Christ, when God first established the church, we read in Acts 1:8: "But you will receive power when the Holy Spirit has come upon you; and you shall be My witnesses both in Jerusalem, and in all Judea and Samaria, and even to the remotest part of the earth."

As Paul writes in his letter to the Romans, "How then will they call on Him in whom they have not believed? How will they believe in Him whom they have not heard? And how will they hear without [someone to tell them]?" (Romans 10:14).

There are many methods of reaching people with the gospel.

As a young believer at Arizona State University, I worked in the newsroom of our student newspaper. Every spring a husband and wife evangelistic team that practiced "confrontational evangelism" would

CHAPTER THREE

appear like clockwork on Cady Mall at ASU, and hundreds of students would gather to laugh, mock, taunt and sometimes listen to the preachers. As a young college student, I wasn't sure about everything they said but I admired two things about them—their fervor and courage in proclaiming the gospel to skeptical college students (the couple spent their honeymoon preaching on college campuses), and their showmanship and ability to hold an audience. As to their technique, I was intrigued but not sure it was very effective. And like most Christians in the audience, some of their "stronger" statements (condemnations) caused me to cringe.

Their annual appearance was the subject of much debate and discussion among newsroom staff, particularly among the sizable number of Christians on our staff. It seemed like the consensus among Christians on staff was that these preachers were an embarrassment, hurtful to the cause of Christ, and not "loving" enough in reaching college students. The fear was that they would drive skeptics further away from the Lord.

I'll never forget a moment in the newsroom when one of the upperclassmen, a quiet, thoughtful, mild-mannered young man who rarely partook in newsroom debates, decided to speak up. I wasn't taking notes, but here's the essence of what he shared:

> I just thought I would let you know that I am a follower of Jesus today because of those preachers. I had plenty of friends over the years 'share Christ' with me gently, befriend me, gently direct me toward Jesus, invite me to ministry events, and while I was appreciative of their concern for my soul, I wasn't very interested in Christianity. But two years ago I was walking across Cady Mall and heard one of the preachers yelling that I would spend eternity in a 'LAKE ... OF ... FIRE!' unless I repented and put my trust in Jesus. I was so shaken and angered that I went back to my dorm room and grabbed a Bible someone had given me and started reading it ... and discovered they were right. So I put my

faith in Jesus and have walked with Him ever since. But I don't think I would ever have come to faith unless someone had confronted me in that way.

That was all he said, but it had a profound effect on the conversation. Later, I came to understand that perhaps we should celebrate the richness and diversity of the ways in which God has equipped each of us to reach the world for Christ, rather than impose formulas or techniques on everyone. Frankly, the supernatural work of God in reaching individual human hearts is so miraculous and mysterious that I'm thankful He not only allows us to participate in His work, but He also so often blesses our flawed, halting attempts to convey our faith to others.

I'm thankful so many different people, using their unique gifts, are so compelled by love for others that they are willing to pray, share, befriend, serve and even confront others with the truth of who God is and what He has done for them and for all of us. As the Apostle Paul wrote:

> For though I am free from all men, I have made myself a slave to all, so that I may win more. To the Jews I became as a Jew, so that I might win Jews; to those who are under the Law, as under the Law though not being myself under the Law, so that I might win those who are under the Law; to those who are without law, as without law, though not being without the law of God but under the law of Christ, so that I might win those who are without law. To the weak I became weak, that I might win the weak; *I have become all things to all men, so that I may by all means save some.* I do all things for the sake of the gospel, so that I may become a fellow partaker of it (1 Corinthians 9:19–23; emphasis added).

Some might argue that a community of Christian believers like ACU provides few evangelistic opportunities. But that misses the point. ACU is meant to be a place of preparation, of training along-

CHAPTER THREE

side fellow believers. No football team scores touchdowns while sitting in the locker room, getting pumped up and reviewing strategy on a chalkboard. But that time of preparation is critical to success on the field.

At the same time, we know with hundreds of new students each year there will always be some incoming ACU students who professed faith in Christ during their application and recruiting process who may not have a full understanding of the gospel. I have personally met multiple Southwestern College graduates going back to the 1960s and 1970s who tell me they were not in fact Christians when they arrived on campus at a Bible college, but quickly came to faith in Jesus and now have spent decades serving the Lord. We know that still happens today, so at the beginning of each semester we provide multiple opportunities for "gospel clarity" decisions.

But the truth is, no students who come to ACU have already "arrived" when it comes to their faith. They all have been influenced —as we all have—by a culture full of contrary worldviews and the messages of the world. ACU challenges students to go deeper, to learn God's truth more deeply and apply it in their own lives more fully. Living out our faith and aligning more closely with God's truth is a process for each of us.

Our Bible curriculum prepares all students with a foundation of Bible classes that include Old and New Testament surveys, along with classes in theology and apologetics. Whether they are new to the faith or grew up in the church, we want all students to have a comprehensive understanding of the Bible and the gospel. Our prayer is that every ACU graduate is "ready to make a defense to everyone who asks you to give an account for the hope that is in you…" (1 Peter 3:15).

At the same time, while ACU is indeed a place of preparation, it is not meant to isolate or insulate students from the culture and the world. In fact, isolating students from worldly influence is impossible today—not when the culture is all around us and as close as the phone in our pockets. But at ACU we provide many opportunities to serve and engage those who do not have a relationship with Jesus, from missions trips available during breaks in the school year, to service opportunities locally. There are many ways for ACU students to serve and share the love of Christ in our community.

The slogan for the old Southwestern College was "intentionally Christian." It was certainly accurate. But in many ways, it was self-focused. It was a statement about who we are on the inside. The new vision, "Transforming Culture with Truth," is outwardly focused, drawing us toward engagement with people outside ACU in the culture and the world.

That change was by design. ACU is a place to prepare to engage the world with biblical truth, and students will have opportunities in their daily life to do that even while attending school. We want to avoid having our students become trapped in a "Christian bubble," internally focused on campus activity with no engagement in the outside community.

In His Sermon on the Mount, Jesus said, "You are the light of the world. A city set on a hill cannot be hidden; nor does anyone light a lamp and put it under a basket, but on the lampstand, and it gives light to all who are in the house. Let your light shine before men in such a way that they may see your good works, and glorify your Father who is in heaven" (Matthew 5:14–16).

We don't want the gospel message to be hidden. Even as we prepare to engage the world, our emphasis on evangelism at ACU reminds us that our light can shine even now in a way that leads others to Jesus.

Be devoted…to prayer without ceasing

> Rejoice always, pray without ceasing, give thanks in all circumstances; for this is the will of God in Christ Jesus for you.
>
> 1 Thessalonians 5:16

The admonition to "pray without ceasing" seems one of the most

CHAPTER THREE

daunting in the New Testament.

For me, it means doing my best to stay in constant conversation with God throughout my day. Recognizing His presence at all times, I try to speak with the Lord throughout the day about anything I am thinking or doing, asking for help, guidance, comfort, encouragement, thanking Him for every good thing, and praising Him for His faithfulness and mercy. One thing we learn when we try to remain in a constant attitude of prayer is this—if we can ever truly master praying "without ceasing" it becomes very difficult to sin. Sinning against God while you are talking to Him is not easy!

Over the past two decades I've been able to speak at dozens of prayer gatherings, often on the National Day of Prayer—the first Thursday in May. In that time, I've watched a modern prayer movement develop, accelerate and mature.

In the past it seemed the schedule at public events marking the National Day of Prayer was filled with speeches about prayer, instead of prayer itself. In recent years this has changed, and the focus of prayer gatherings increasingly has become actual prayer time, individually and corporately. The emphasis on praying for leaders in government and the community is welcome, and consistent with Scripture, as we are told to pray "first" for those in authority (1 Timothy 2:1–2).

Shortly after the terrorist attacks on 9/11 in 2001, I was asked to serve as a founding advisory board member for the Presidential Prayer Team, an idea that was birthed in Arizona. Over the next few years millions of Americans joined the team and committed to pray for the President and national leaders. To help me remember to pray for the President regularly, I started using certain techniques and triggers. One of the easiest is this—anytime I would hear the National Anthem, usually at a sporting event, I would take those few minutes to lift up the President of the United States and other national leaders in prayer. I have continued this practice for U.S. Presidents and governmental leaders of both political parties for the past few decades. They all need prayer! I often add to it by praying for our nation and our soldiers, and

I ask God in His mercy to turn our nation back to Him.

For many Christians, even leaders in churches and parachurch ministries, there is a temptation to fall into a pattern of what my wife, Dr. Tracy Munsil, once referred to as the "nod to God"—the quick, perfunctory "Lord, thank you for this day and this opportunity to serve you; now please bless the stuff we were already gonna do in Jesus' name. Amen." While this is better than no prayer at all, it is not the deep communion with our Creator described so often in Scripture and modeled by Jesus.

In the busyness of life, it is quite possible for Christian leaders, even pastors, to be so busy serving and working that they leave out the essential element of communion with God—honoring Him for His goodness, and asking for His help. One pastor tells of spending years as a "prayerless pastor." Only after encountering God in a new and significant way through a commitment to prayer that engaged the entire church did God begin to pour our growth, conversions, baptisms and church plants on that congregation. Other than prayer, they were doing nothing else that was different.

We learn from Luke's description that Jesus "would withdraw to desolate places and pray." On one occasion He "went out to the mountain to pray, and all night he continued in prayer to God" (Luke 5:16, 6:12). It is painful to compare so much of what passes for our prayer life in modern times with the obvious time and dedication Jesus spent pursuing relationship with His Father.

Prayer is an immediate response for many of us in times of trial. But it can be so much more. "Do not be anxious about anything, but *in everything* [emphasis added] by prayer and supplication with thanksgiving let your requests be made known to God" (Philippians 4:6; emphasis added).

I have seen the power of prayer during my lifetime on countless occasions, although I am certain in many ways, we will not understand just how important prayer was in our life until we reach heaven. In His mercy, God has given me just a glimpse of ways in which

CHAPTER THREE

my relationship with Christ today was an answer to the prayers of many. Not just godly parents, but without knowing it for sure, I am confident the many believers in my extended family going back generations—many of whom were pastors—prayed for grandchildren, great-grandchildren, and future generations yet unborn, even as I pray today for my children, their future children, and generations beyond.

More specifically, I am aware of a group of men and women who started gathering near campus in the late 1970s to pray for an awakening at Arizona State University. These Christians were concerned about the increasing pull of sexual immorality, drunkenness, drug use and atheism on campus, sparked in part by the decision of the administration to allow—under the guise of free speech—the public, free showing by a fraternity of a pornographic film in a large science classroom on campus. (This was in the days when hard-core pornography was illegal, there was no Internet, and the only way to view pornography was to be at least 21 years old and to go to an "adult" bookstore in a seedy part of town.)

So these leaders gathered regularly and prayed for an awakening on campus. But they were specific in their prayers. They prayed that God would raise up Christian leadership on campus in student government and at the newspaper, the *State Press*. Specifically, they prayed that Christians would be selected as the President and Vice President of student government and as top editors of the newspaper, or that students selected for those positions would come to faith in Christ.

My wife and I were both part of how God answered those specific prayers. About five years after those prayer gatherings began, Tracy came to faith in Christ while she was Editor of the *State Press*. One year later I renewed my commitment to the Lord and became serious about daily Bible reading and prayer while I was Editor. During the year I led ASU's daily newspaper, I was blessed to be able to gather weekly with the President and Vice President of ASU's student body, along with another top newspaper editor—all Christians—as the four of us together prayed for God to move on ASU's campus among the students we served. In just a few years of faithful prayer, this prayer group was able to see God answer in a powerful way on the ASU campus.

More than 20 years later, I was traveling with an acquaintance, the father of one of my son's high school friends. We were all headed to Denver to visit Colorado Christian University, where both boys were recruited and eventually played college baseball. I found out during that trip that the father of my son's friend—a pastor—was actually one of the men in that prayer group! I had heard of the prayer group but never had a chance to speak to someone who could confirm the details of how they prayed and how God answered those prayers.

Many years later, I would still see this gentleman around the campus of Arizona Christian University. His name is Dr. Steven Rutt, an associate professor of Biblical Studies at ACU. I remain thankful that Dr. Rutt was faithful in prayer 40 years ago, when he regularly prayed for God to transform student editors at ASU's campus newspaper, and that God answered those prayers. Every time I would see Dr. Rutt on campus, I would be reminded of the faithfulness of God in answering prayer.

It seems awakenings are always preceded by prayer movements, usually among young people. I remain hopeful about the future in part because of the commitment to fervent and frequent prayer I see among so many passionate Christ followers in our student body and among young people generally. My greatest hope and prayer for the students of Arizona Christian University is that they will play a significant part in what God is doing to awaken their generation to the truths of Christianity.

Evangelism, Prayer, and Cultural Transformation

I believe the students, faculty and staff of ACU have been brought here for a purpose, and for something larger and more significant than a college degree.

Many years ago, I picked up a book about a nation described as

CHAPTER THREE

"on the verge of moral disintegration."[1] What did that nation and culture look like?

- The leader of this nation lived in open adultery, and part of the normal educational process was to teach young men the art of seduction.
- Marriage was "as much ridiculed by our young ladies as it used to be by young men" and was generally considered inconvenient—most young people chose to live together rather than get married.
- The moral laxity was reflected in the entertainment culture—popular entertainment was sexually provocative and exploitative; theaters were filled with "lewdness" and nudity, and books were designed to provide cheap titillation.
- Meanwhile, "the nation found itself enmeshed in the twin snares of drink and gambling." Every class of society suffered from drunkenness. Public gambling houses were officially licensed; one writer said that "society was one vast casino." "To make matters worse, the Government itself at once exploited and inflamed the universal desire for gain by sponsoring state lotteries."
- Statistics on violent crime soared. Prisons were overcrowded and tended to harden prisoners rather than reform them.
- Gangs of "hooligans" roamed the city streets, clashing with their rivals or assaulting unsuspecting citizens.
- Most of the people of this nation were completely indifferent to the claims of Christianity, and according to the book, "little of Christianity is now to be found among Christians themselves." In other words, even most Christians did not live according to a biblical worldview.

Sound familiar? Sound at all like the United States today? The book I was reading is called *The Burning Heart: John Wesley, Evangelist*[2] and it was written more than a half-century ago, in 1967—long before there were clear parallels with what was happening in the United States. Even more shocking, the nation being described was Great Britain during the first half of the 18th Century, the nation into which John Wesley, his brother Charles Wesley, and George Whitefield and other evangelists were born.

As we think about what God might have in store for us at ACU, I'm reminded again of the difference made by a few students, staff and faculty at a small college in England three centuries ago, who started to gather to read the Bible and pray. This group was founded by the Wesley brothers and later joined by Whitefield.

They were part of a Christian college community in a culture that was shockingly post-Christian, as described by the book. Even the future pastors at that school would sometimes mock this small group as they gathered in the college chapel to read Scripture and pray, first one night a week, then two, then four, then every night, for an hour, then two hours, then three.[3]

But their fervency began to influence others at the college. They began to move into the community, visiting and ministering to prisoners and taking care of the poor. And they began to speak and preach about God in their community, and then around the country, and eventually even in colonial America. And they ignited a spark in England that turned into a flame in America that led to the Great Awakening—a time when millions of people worldwide turned to a relationship with God through Jesus Christ.

As people turned to Christ they were changed, and the culture changed with them. Families and marriages were restored, as the hearts of fathers were turned to their children; crime was reduced, people stopped getting drunk and returned to church by the millions.

All of the social issues England was dealing with were affected by this awakening. As a direct result, Christian leaders like William Wilberforce rose up in government and fought to prohibit slavery, and

CHAPTER THREE

laws were changed.

Popular entertainment and literature, playwrights and authors, began to write redemptive works based on truth. Businesses began to operate with integrity and charity. Hospitals and orphanages and shelters were built to help the most vulnerable.

Historians are quite clear—that little prayer group at Oxford and its consequences had a transformative effect on that entire nation. And the awakening that began there spread to the New World and affected even the founding of the American republic.

That's what we are talking about when we talk about transforming culture with truth.

Hundreds of years ago, at a small Christian college, a handful of people decided to gather to pray and read Scripture together. They lived in a culture and a nation a lot like ours today—a culture that had almost completely forgotten God. Yet God enabled them to transform culture with truth, and the world was changed.

Could it happen again? Could it happen here?

We live today in a world and among a generation where people are lost; they need the transforming power of a personal relationship with Jesus Christ. We live in a culture in desperate need of reformation according to biblical truth.

In the spring and summer of 2020, the combination of a global COVID pandemic, which led to lockdowns and a staggering economy, combined with great political conflict and civic unrest that began with protests over racial injustice—all of these things combined to create a sense of desperation, hopelessness and fear in our nation and the world. These same challenging circumstances created a hunger and an opening for an awakening to the gospel and the truths of Scripture. Prayer rallies, solemn assemblies and a renewed focus on repentance and returning to God may be setting the stage for the awakening that is needed.

In the midst of that, I believe God can use a handful of students at this little (but growing!) college in the desert to bring transformation, first in our lives and our community, and then an awakening to the world around us. Will you pray for that with me?

Princeton University of the Ivy League was the first college in America founded out of the Great Awakening that began at Oxford. This is the prayer still chiseled onto the wall of Princeton's chapel. As the spiritual heir of these originally Christian institutions of higher learning, let's pray this prayer for Arizona Christian University:

> O Eternal God
> The Creator and Preserver
> Of all mankind we beseech Thee
> To bestow upon this university
> Thy Manifold gifts of grace
> Thy Truth to those who teach
> Thy Laws to those who learn
> Thy Wisdom to those who administer
> And Thy steadfastness to all
> Who bear her name
> Bind us together by these
> Gracious influences of Thy Spirit
> Into that fellowship
> Which can never fail the company
> Of Jesus Christ our Lord
> Amen.[4]

Chapter Notes

1 A. Skevington Wood, *The Burning Heart, John Wesley: Evangelist* (Grand Rapids, MI: Wm. B. Eerdmans Publishing Company, 1967). All following quotes (pp. 64-65) are taken from this work.

2 A reprint edition is available: A. Skevington Wood, *The Burning Heart, John Wesley: Evangelist* (Darden Prarie, MO: Emeth Press, 2007).

3 "The Life of John Wesley by John Telford – Chapter 5," Wesley Center Online, 2011, http://wesley.nnu.edu/john-wesley/the-life-of-john-wesley-

CHAPTER THREE

by-john-telford/the-life-of-john-wesley-by-john-telford-chapter-5/.

4   Richard Stillwell, *The Chapel of Princeton University* (Princeton, NJ: Princeton University Press, 2020), 140.

FOUR

~

Arizona Christian University shall:
…Be committed to loving God with all our heart and soul, mind and strength, by pursuing excellence in spiritual formation, academics, athletics and extracurricular activities, doing all for the glory of God.

What is it about lawyers?

Q: "What do you call a thousand lawyers at the bottom of the ocean?"

A: "A good start."

Q: "Why won't sharks eat lawyers?"

A: "Professional courtesy."

You may have heard that Saint Peter decided to build a wall between Heaven and Hell. Naturally, he approached the Devil and asked him to help.

"Forget it," said the Devil. "You want the wall, you build it."

"Okay, I will, but I'm going to send you a bill to pay for half of it," said Saint Peter.

"I won't pay it," said the Devil.

"Then I'll sue you," said Saint Peter.

The Devil smiled. "Where are you going to find a lawyer?"

You get the idea. Admittedly, I'm not always a fan of fellow members of the Bar.

For many years I played softball in a Lawyers' League. I felt sorry for the umpires the whole time. Every call the umpire made turned into an argument.

We certainly need some good attorneys, but why are they so often the punch line in jokes and the bad guys in so many stories? Even in the Bible!

Jesus said, "Woe to you scribes and lawyers." Since I have been a journalist (scribe) and an attorney, I pretty much have the professions Jesus condemned covered.

As recorded in Luke 10:25–27, a troublesome lawyer came to Jesus with what he thought was the catch-all question:

> And a lawyer stood up to put him to the test, saying, "Teacher, what shall I do to inherit eternal life?"
>
> And He said to him: "What is written in the Law? How does it read to you?"
>
> The lawyer responded, reciting from the Old Testament: "You shall love the Lord your God with all your heart, and with all your soul, and with all your strength, and with all your mind; and your neighbor as yourself."
>
> And He said to him: "You have answered correctly; do this and you will live."

On another occasion, Jesus was asked which commandment was the greatest:

> Jesus answered, "The foremost is, 'Hear, O Israel! The Lord our God is one Lord; and you shall love the Lord your God with all your heart, and with all your soul, and with all your mind, and with all your strength.' The second is this, 'You shall love your neighbor as yourself.' There is no other commandment greater than these." The scribe said to Him, "Right, Teacher; You have truly stated that He is One, and there is no one else besides Him; and to love Him with all the heart and with all the understanding and with all the strength, and to love one's neighbor as himself, is much more than all burnt offerings and sacrifices." When Jesus saw that he had answered intelligently, He said to him, "You are not

CHAPTER FOUR

far from the kingdom of God." After that, no one would venture to ask Him any more questions (Mark 12:28–34).

I love that—Jesus was so persuasive that the lawyers and religious leaders trying to trip him up just gave up and stopped asking questions.

I've often thought that this foundational passage speaks directly to what should be the goal of every Christian university.

In a Christian university, loving God "with all of your *heart and soul*" speaks to the importance and significance of *helping students grow and mature as followers of Jesus Christ*. So as an institution, we should make student spiritual growth a vital element of every student's university experience, and we should go all out to pursue excellence in our walk with God.

In a Christian university, loving God "with all of your *mind*" speaks to the importance of *pursuing excellence in our academic programs*. It calls our students to work hard in the classroom, and to recognize they are bringing glory to God by giving their all to becoming the best students they can be. It calls our faculty and administration and staff to build strong, effective academic programs that prepare graduates well for successful careers.

Loving God "with all your *strength*" seems like a great way to describe our *extracurricular activities and programs*. The world needs strong Christian leaders. Whether it is the discipline, preparation, perseverance, and teamwork involved in participating in intercollegiate athletics and intramurals, or the hard work and sweat involved in cleaning up the yards and homes of the elderly in our neighborhoods as part of a service project, or the dedication to practice required to become an excellent musician, vocalist, or worship team member—extracurricular opportunities at ACU provide students with multiple opportunities to "love God with all [their] strength."

Here is the important thing to remember about this passage: What Jesus described as the two greatest commandments—loving God and loving your neighbor—are deeply embedded in the mission, vision and Core Commitments of Arizona Christian University.

When the school changed its name from Southwestern College to Arizona Christian University, students voted on a new athletic team name and mascot. Previously, the school had been the Eagles—like 93 other colleges across the United States! Zeke the Eagle was the mascot and, at least in my experience at the school, Zeke's appearances on campus were about as rare as wins for Southwestern College Eagle athletic teams.[1]

The winner of the team name vote was the Firestorm, completely unique in higher education in America. An actual "firestorm" is a conflagration so intense that it creates its own windstorm, and our prayer is that ACU would spark intense spiritual fires among college students. We also discovered that Firestorm is an obscure DC Comics character who was created out of a nuclear explosion and has a split personality.

Seriously—check this dude out[2]:

Scary, right? But that's not who the students chose as a mascot. They voted for a phoenix bird as the mascot, I think partially based on our location in the greater Phoenix area, and also because of some comparisons between the mythological phoenix bird being reborn and rising from the ashes and our rebirth as followers of Jesus. Anyway, here's a photo of our phoenix bird mascot, named Stormin' Norman by yet another student vote.

Stormin' Norman patrols the new ACU campus in 2019.

Maybe with the phoenix bird students were thinking about the rebirth of Arizona Christian University from the ashes of Southwestern College. Or maybe it was prophetic. Little did we know when that vote was taken, just a few years later ACU would be reborn yet again on a much larger campus in the Phoenix suburb of Glendale—on a former World War II air base, and out of the ashes of the failure of the Thunderbird School of Global Management.

That's another part of the miracle of ACU. When the highly respected Thunderbird School of Global Management (TSGM) faced financial challenges in 2014, my alma mater Arizona State University stepped in and rescued the school. But after four years of operation on the Glendale campus, ASU determined to move TSGM to a new building at its downtown campus.

Meanwhile at our landlocked Cactus Road campus in north Phoenix, after years of growth, we were simply out of room. Without sufficient parking, classroom space or athletic facilities, our rate of growth was dwindling and we could not easily invest in necessary new buildings with such a tiny campus footprint. To continue growing, we needed more classrooms, more parking, and in reality, more land. Recognizing this problem early in my tenure as President, for years I had been actively looking for ways to either enlarge our current campus or find a new location that had more room. Despite some near misses, all of those efforts had been stymied. As it turned out, God was just setting up a miracle!

As soon as I heard about ASU's decision to close the Thunderbird Glendale campus, that very night I emailed ASU President Michael Crow, explained our situation, and asked about their plans for the historic campus. He responded almost immediately that they had some preliminary ideas, but nothing was decided yet; in fact, he said "all things are possible." Of course, right away I thought of Matthew 19:26: "And looking at them Jesus said to them, 'With people this is impossible, but with God all things are possible.'" And honestly, that's how it seemed with our human eyes—an impossibility.

That led to 11 months and hundreds of hours of confidential negotiations with Arizona State University's top financial, real estate and legal professionals, and lots of prayer. And with President Crow's strong support, it all culminated in an announcement in November of 2018 that we were trading campuses! ASU needed to sell land to pay for its new TSGM building downtown and would need to demolish the academic buildings in Glendale. But the value of the land on our 20-acre campus in north Phoenix was roughly equal to the 68 acres of land in Glendale, so the exchange made sense for ASU. They could generate as much funding by selling the Cactus campus. Just as importantly, the campus swap enabled ASU to leave a historic academic campus in place in Glendale for its intended educational purposes. The City of Glendale was thrilled. Glendale Mayor Jerry Weiers, an old political ally and former state legislator during my days as a Christian attorney fighting for conservative values at the Capitol, was a huge advocate for the deal and for ACU's decision to "go west."

CHAPTER FOUR

I will never forget the feeling as we waited, with an entire gymnasium full of students, faculty, staff, Trustees and friends, for the transaction to officially be recorded with the county. I heard later that many in the stands that day were speculating that Arizona Christian University was about to join that sad list of small colleges who have been forced to close due to the challenging economic circumstances facing higher education in America.

ACU students react to a video showing ACU's new campus at a special chapel on November 14, 2018.

Instead, with the last notes of Switchfoot's "Dare You to Move" echoing through the gym, I was able to share the amazing miracle God had done in our midst. Lyrics from that song had particular meaning for me. A decade earlier, as a Trustee of then-Southwestern College, I had been driving around campus praying for the students and future of the school at a time of great uncertainty when that song came on. And these lines leaped out at me: "The tension is here … Between who you are and who you could be … Between how it is and how it should be …". I was overcome with emotion as I sensed God telling me that this little college had so much more potential for His Kingdom, and that I might have a role to play in it. At the time I was actively being recruited to run for political office and was leaning that direction. But weeks later, when the Board of Trustees asked me to step in as interim President, I remembered that moment in prayer and accepted the role for two years. Or so I thought.

Nearly a decade later I was announcing God's miracle provision of a new campus. We canceled classes for the rest of the day and bused all of our students about nine miles west to the new campus, where we were joined by President Crow and other dignitaries from ASU and the City of Glendale. With nearly 1,000 people and local media in the Events Center, we thanked God for this unexpected blessing and dedicated our new campus to the Lord.

For ACU, it was a game-changing miracle. We not only more than tripled the size of our campus, but also more than tripled the academic buildings, classroom space, parking and residence hall rooms. Finally, room to grow! And just another sign of God's blessing on our mission—and a historic step closer to ACU closing the gap "between how [the University] is and how it should be."

ACU's campus as it looked in the early 1940s while serving as an Army air base where thousands of pilots were trained for action in World War II.

The historic Glendale campus has a unique and unusual history that ties well into the mission of ACU. Back when there were patriots in Hollywood, with great foresight a group of producers and actors including Jimmy Stewart purchased the land and established an air strip, then leased the land to the Army Air Corps in 1941. This was

CHAPTER FOUR

prior to Pearl Harbor and the entry of the United States into World War II. Over the next four years, thousands of pilots were trained for military action on this campus in the middle of the Arizona desert. A monument to these pilots still stands on campus. The centerpiece of the new campus is the Tower, which is the original World War II airfield flight tower, completely restored and updated in 2012 and now functioning as ACU's Student Union.

We have challenged the students to consider the heritage of this campus—that we daily walk in the footsteps of heroes who were trained to fight and defeat the evils of Nazi fascism and anti-Semitism in Hitler's Germany, and the aggressively expansionist and brutally militaristic Japanese Empire of that era. In the same way, as we consider the forces of evil in our world today—destructive ideologies that ruin lives and lead people away from the truth—at ACU we are preparing men and women with a great education and the hope of the gospel to transform lives and culture. We love the parallels with this new place God gave to our University—a place of training and equipping to fight evil.

And we have embraced some fun with the air base history through the introduction of the Firestorm Air Raid Siren at our dedication chapel in 2019 and at appropriate moments throughout the year, such as when the ACU football team scores a touchdown! Inscribed on the Siren, a thoughtful gift from the Andy and Amy Unkefer family, is the following from Isaiah 29:6: "The LORD Almighty will come with thunder and earthquake and great noise, with windstorm, rainstorms and Firestorm!"

So, a new name, Arizona Christian University. A new vision to "transform culture with truth." A new team name, the Firestorm. A new mascot, a phoenix bird, Stormin' Norman. And finally, a new campus in Glendale, that will enable us to fulfill our mission and vision with excellence.

When Arizona Christian University put together its strategic plan a few years back, we determined that we would use the *F-I-R-E* from

Firestorm as an acronym to clarify our distinctive and unique vision for ACU:

F is for FAITH.
I is for INFLUENCE.
R is for RELATIONSHIP.
E is for EXCELLENCE.

FAITH: Our faith in Christ is what unites us at ACU, and the reason we seek to love God with all of our heart, soul, mind and strength.

Since ACU began as a Bible college in 1960, training Christian students for ministries and professional occupations has always been its purpose. In the early days of the college, the focus was almost exclusively on vocational ministries, training pastors, music and worship leaders, missionaries and Bible study teachers. Today the focus on preparing Christians for leadership positions remains, but the vision for their engagement has expanded to include other vocations where strong Bible-believing Christians are needed in leadership.

When I joined the Board of Trustees of then–Southwestern College in 2003, one of the recurring topics of discussion was, "How do we keep this college from losing its Christian purpose?" We were all familiar with the Christ-centered, Bible-focused foundation of the Ivy League schools centuries ago compared to their secular purpose today, and we were also familiar with even more modern examples of Christian universities losing identity and purpose.

A book, *The Dying of the Light: The Disengagement of Colleges and Universities from Their Christian Churches,* was written by James Tunstead Burtchaell as a case study of many of these institutions.[3]

I will never forget a board meeting conference call with the late Reno Hoff, the very successful president of Corban University in Salem, Oregon. With his vast experience in Christian higher education, President Hoff explained to us on the Trustee board what he believed was the turning point. He said most Christian colleges began

CHAPTER FOUR

to lose their faith-based purpose not because of a change in the Trustee board, not because of a change in the President, or even a change in the faculty. He said in his experience, Christian universities lost their way when they changed admissions policies to admit any student, even those with no profession of faith in Jesus Christ.

He explained in his autobiography, *The Reno Hoff Story*, published in 2013 shortly before his death:

> This is why it is so important to keep our mission to educate Christians only; I believe a school will drift from its original mission if it accepts unbelievers.
>
> In his thoroughly researched book, *The Dying of the Light*, James Burtchaell catalogs the sad history of 17 American Christian colleges and universities that have left the faith….
>
> Christian institutions that eventually reject Christianity all have one thing in common. They start drifting when they allow unbelievers to attend their colleges. Eventually the mission, vision and core values change to accommodate the unbelievers, and in the end the schools completely reject Christianity.
>
> Some Christian institutions say they let unbelievers in to evangelize them. What actually happens is that, in a sense, the unbelievers do the evangelizing. Slowly, they convert the institution to their way of thinking.
>
> At Corban, we wholeheartedly believe in evangelism, but we are training our students and graduates to do the outreach. It's not the school's job to do it. I believe this is the reason we are growing faster than a number of institutions that don't share our mission.[4]

Even in the last few years, I've seen the wisdom of President Hoff's observations. I have visited self-described "Christian" schools where students (and even faculty sometimes) openly mock Christians on campus, and where destructive and unbiblical moral decisions are promoted openly by students. At one institution where chapel is still required, a tour guide for prospective students and parents not only made fun of the chapel requirement, but also described all the various ways students could avoid attending or participating in chapel.

That is not the case for every Christian university that admits non-Christians; in my view, some have done better than others at maintaining and prioritizing their Christian purpose. But the danger is real of a loss of Christian commitment, especially in a culture that is becoming increasingly hostile to Christianity. It is my prayer that those universities open to all will continue to advance the gospel, continue to evangelize nonbelieving students, and resist the pull to abandon their Christian purpose. For Christian universities that have already drifted, this will require a board and president with the courage to recommit to teaching according to a counter-culture conservative, biblical worldview, while also making the necessary staffing and faculty changes to enable the university to fulfill its original purpose.

We know that even at Arizona Christian University, despite coaches, recruiters and admissions team members emphasizing that a personal Christian commitment is a condition of admission, sometimes unbelieving students slip through the process. At times they are able to hide that they do not have a serious commitment to Christ. In some cases, perhaps they did not have enough spiritual background to even understand what they were missing. This can be discouraging to mature Christian students who come to ACU expecting every student to share their deeply rooted faith and understanding of the Bible. I always try to remind these students, especially early in the semester, that we need mature Christian students to set the standard and help us disciple students who are newer in the faith. Part of Christian maturity is understanding, having patience with, praying for, and encouraging others to draw closer to God. But we have not relaxed our admissions standards. Students who seem genuinely disinterested or opposed to the things of God should not be at Arizona Christian University.

CHAPTER FOUR

Generally speaking, in these hard cases one of two things happens. Many times the student comes to faith in Christ and becomes an amazing testimony of God's power to transform. We've had dozens of baptisms every year I've been at ACU as students get serious about owning their faith and decide to make a public declaration of their commitment to Christ. In a few cases, the story of how students deceived the university in order to be admitted to ACU as unbelievers has now become a part of the testimony of their conversion to Christ. As I've said, I have met many alumni who committed their lives to Christ after they arrived at Southwestern College/ACU and went on to enjoy many years of faithful Christian service. Some happily tell of their conversion during chapel at Southwestern College in the 1970s, and their involvement in full-time ministry ever since.

On other occasions, students who are not serious about Christ will realize we meant what we told them during the admissions process. We expect them to follow Jesus and we will hold them accountable to conduct themselves according to biblical standards and to grow in their Christian faith. If they continue to resist the gospel and discipleship, they typically make the decision to transfer, and on some occasions their disruptive conduct forces ACU to separate them from the University.

But there is a significant difference in the makeup of a student body between occasional unbelieving students getting admitted despite our admissions policies, versus the abandonment of any faith requirement as has occurred at so many Christian colleges and universities. As President Hoff warned, removing the Christian faith requirement for prospective students nearly always results in a college ultimately losing the Christian purpose for which it was formed. That will not happen at ACU.

For more than a half-century, ACU has been dedicated to preparing Christians for leadership roles in the church and the community. Our "iron-sharpening-iron" approach is also vital to developing Christian leaders in our culture. The requirement that ACU students have a testimony of faith in Christ, and our commitment to the spiritual growth of our students, is the reason faith is the first element listed in our *F-I-R-E* acronym.

INFLUENCE: Jesus said the second commandment after loving God is to "love your neighbor as yourself." Because we desire to "love our neighbor," we want to bring the life-giving principles of God to the world and culture around us. Jesus told us to be "salt and light," to engage the world with His love and His teachings. We do so because we know the consequences for individuals and cultures that reject God and His ways are catastrophic. Bringing Christian influence into the world will be discussed at greater length in Chapter Seven.

RELATIONSHIP: We demonstrate our love for our neighbor through relationships and through community. The relationships we develop in this Christian covenant community are a significant priority for ACU, and many of our programs—and even the way we teach—are designed to enhance relationship.

This strong sense of community is one of the most consistent elements of our University's history. Invariably, when I speak to alumni of our school, they talk about the relationships they developed with faculty, administrators, and of course their fellow students. Close relationships developed during college nearly always extend throughout the decades, and sometimes for the rest of your life. Many students end up getting married to fellow students, and the chances for a happy and successful marriage are so much greater when husband and wife are not "unequally yoked" but instead share a common Christian faith and purpose.

So many elements of this life and world pass away, but two things are eternal: our relationship with God and our relationships with each other. Since we're going to be together throughout eternity, we might as well start now, by being committed to building and developing supportive, encouraging relationships today in this Christian community at ACU.

Our commitment to building relationships within the body of

CHAPTER FOUR

Christ, and within our Christian community at ACU, is one reason we are so committed to opposing racism and injustice. This commitment began long before the marches and protests during the summer of 2020 drew attention to the unjust killings of unarmed black men and women in our country. When I arrived as President of ACU in 2010, our student population did not reflect the diversity of the body of Christ in our community or nation. Over the next decade we strategically sought to pursue and welcome Christian students from the African American and Hispanic communities. By 2020, ACU had become much more reflective of the community of Christians in our state and nation, with 29 percent Hispanic and 16 percent African American populations on campus. This was not an accident. It was the result of strategic enrollment decisions based on the principle that you cannot transform culture with biblical truth if you are only graduating students from one segment of our Christian community.

One of the great joys of the past decade has been seeing so many barriers broken down at a conservative Christian university, as students of all backgrounds, races, ethnicities, family circumstances and from more than 30 states and 20 foreign countries begin to realize together that in the family of God, we are all brothers and sisters. What unites us is so much greater than the ways the world seeks to divide us. That was the theme of a #UnitedinPrayer event in September of 2020. Students, staff, faculty and administration came together to pray for an end to racism, injustice and unequal treatment under the law, to repent of our past failures as a people to live up to these biblical principles, to forgive one another, and to pledge to each other at ACU that we would "love one another" and live in community as followers of Jesus without regard to race. Our theme verse was Acts 17:26: "And He hath made of one blood all nations of men to dwell on all the face of the earth...."

By emphasizing the biblical view that all nations and all peoples come from one man, or one blood, at ACU we can seek unity in ways the secular world cannot. We strive to remind each other that we are all part of the same body, the same family, and that we are each part of one another. And race should never be an obstacle or a differentiator in the family of God (Romans 12:5). Seeing lifelong friendships and sometimes marriages form at ACU without regard to race, ethnicity or nationality is a gratifying experience that can provide hope and an example to the world.

Jesus told us that "By this everyone will know that you are my disciples, if you love one another" (John 13:35). By building a community centered around Jesus and by emphasizing our love for one another, we can demonstrate to a hopeless, angry, aggrieved, divided, often unjust and unfair world that there is a better way—the way of the cross. That is why building "Relationship" will always be one of the core values of Arizona Christian University.

EXCELLENCE: We are asked by Jesus to love God with all of our heart, soul, mind and strength. That speaks to going all out, and being "all in."

Colossians 3:23 says, "Whatever you do, do your work heartily, as for the Lord rather than for men." The pursuit of excellence—whether it be in academics, athletics, music, or another extracurricular activity—brings honor and glory to God.

When I coached my kids' teams in youth sports, I liked to remind the players at the beginning of the season that there are many things largely beyond your control in sports—the talent level of the competition, your size and natural athleticism, the calls made by umpires and referees, etc. But there are two things that are completely within your control: your attitude and your effort.

The pursuit of excellence is like that. We all start from different places, with different backgrounds and challenges and abilities, but we can all commit to bringing the right attitude and effort to anything we attempt. Excellence is hard to measure, but it is something we should aspire to, even as we recognize that we often fall short. Knowing that God wants us to do our best and try our hardest should motivate us to pursue excellence in all things. At a university that means making

CHAPTER FOUR

every effort to become the best Christ follower, the best student, the best athlete, the best musician and the best person we can become.

For us at Arizona Christian University, it means striving to constantly improve the educational, relational and spiritual experience for our students. These efforts of many years are starting to pay off in significant ways, and to be recognized by independent objective sources.

In 2017, for the first time in its six decades of existence, ACU was recognized as a "Best College" in the West Region by *U.S. News & World Report,* the "gold standard" of university ratings systems. ACU was ranked a "Best College" in each subsequent year for four straight years, reaching its highest ranking ever in 2020 in the 15-state West region.

At the same time, ACU was selected by *U.S. News & World Report* as the No. 1 Undergraduate Teaching institution in the West! That remarkable achievement was a testimony to our amazing faculty and their commitment to excellence in the classroom. We also were ranked No. 3 in the West for "social mobility," meaning we have been particularly effective at educating first-generation and economically challenged students. ACU has achieved many other high rankings from other organizations in the past few years as a top Christian university, top online university, and best university in the state of Arizona.

These rankings are important because they demonstrate that ACU is not just calling students to be the best they can be. We are also constantly challenging ourselves to improve in all that we do. We want the quality and value of the education we are providing to continue to improve. That's also what motivated our search for a larger campus and better facilities, and why we are constantly raising money to repair, improve and expand campus facilities. ACU is an imperfect institution made up of imperfect people that is constantly seeking to improve in its pursuit of excellence.

1 Corinthians 10:31 says, "… whatever you do, do all to the glory of God." The Academy Award winning film *Chariots of Fire* (1981) is based on a true story that focuses on a British missionary to China

who struggles with pursuing his dream of running in the 1924 Olympics because to do so will delay his missionary pursuits. In a pivotal scene from the movie, he explains to his sister why he is choosing to run in the Olympic Games: "I believe God made me for a purpose, but he also made me fast! And when I run, I feel his pleasure."[5]

God made you for a purpose as well. As Christians, we know how this race ends, and we know what awaits us all in heaven. Good stuff! So, for today, let's pursue Christ and pursue excellence and not leave anything on the playing field of life. As the Scripture teaches, "Make the most of your time, for the days are evil" (Ephesians 5:16).

Chapter Notes

1. For most of Southwestern College's existence, there were very few athletic teams, men's basketball and women's volleyball having the longest heritage. To be fair, there were some pretty good men's basketball teams at the small Christian college level, including one coached by NBA All-Star and future NBA coach and Hall of Famer Paul Westphal in the 1980s, and a Christian college national championship team coached by Steve Morley in the 1990s. In recent years, the athletic program at Arizona Christian University has grown significantly and made great strides, with numerous teams receiving national rankings, playoff opportunities, and scholar-athlete awards at the NAIA level. Opportunities to fund excellence in our athletic program through scholarships and improved facilities are available through the Westphal Athletic Fund. (https://www.arizonachristian.edu/westphalathleticfund/).
2. ©DC Comics. Image accessed at: www.dccomics.com
3. James Tunstead Burtchaell, *The Dying of the Light: The Disengagement of Colleges and Universities from Their Churches* (Grand Rapids, MI: Eerdmans Publishing Co., 1998).
4. Reno Hoff, *The Reno Hoff Story: The First 78 Years: June 1935–June 2013* (n.p.: CreateSpace, 2013), 184.
5. *Chariots of Fire,* directed by Hugh Hudson (Hollywood, CA: Twentieth Century Fox Film Corporation, 1981).

FIVE

~

Arizona Christian University shall:
Teach students to think critically, speak and write clearly and effectively, use technology effectively, develop interpersonal skills, and pursue personal and professional ethics through biblical literacy and integration.

The mission of Arizona Christian University remains to provide "a biblically-integrated, liberal arts education equipping graduates to serve the Lord Jesus Christ in all aspects of life, as leaders of influence and excellence."

The element of our Core Commitments listed above is an expression of our University's historic educational mission and has been in place at ACU as part of our academic goals and assessments for many years.

Arizona Christian University shall: *Teach students to think critically, speak and write clearly and effectively...*

Church choirs seem increasingly to be a thing of the past. That's a shame, because you never know what might come from singing in the choir at your local church. In fact, it was while singing in a choir that I first was invited to be involved at this University.

In the early 1990s I was at a choir practice at Scottsdale Baptist Church when another choir member changed my life. Dr. Shelly Roden[1], who served as Academic Dean at then–Southwestern College, was looking for an adjunct professor to teach a senior capstone course in Christian ethics and decided to ask me.

I'd heard of the college but didn't know where it was. As a young attorney with a big family running a national legal ministry, I didn't have much spare time. But I decided to give it a try, and I quickly came to appreciate the Christ-centered educational focus and the passion, kindness and genuine Christian faith of the students.

When dealing with Christian ethics in the classroom—issues like abortion, human sexuality, war and peace, civil disobedience and capital punishment—it became clear to me that most students had a pretty good grasp of what the "answer" was from the Bible. But none of them had been trained to think critically about the issues or defend their position in an argument.

My college experience involved high-profile positions at Arizona State University, as editor of the daily newspaper and then the leader of a conservative law student organization. From there I had gone on to defend biblical principles as a lawyer in legislative hearings and public debates, including on radio and TV. I was accustomed to defending Christian values and biblical truths in a hostile, secular environment.

I knew the arguments against Christian ethical principles in the culture could be persuasive. The folks making them were usually smart and articulate. Ultimately the arguments are wrong, but there are reasons so many young Christians who've been sheltered from the culture get swept away by false philosophies when they enter the real world.

So, I decided as a professor to challenge my students to think critically, using my legal and debate skills to attack Christian ethical principles. For weeks I would ask provocative questions and provide no answers, challenging the students to defend their beliefs. Many times, frustrated students would approach me after class wanting to know what I really thought, or what the "right answer" was, or how an answer they knew was morally wrong could sound so right.

The goal, of course, was to help students learn to think through

CHAPTER FIVE

the application of biblical principles to difficult issues and to learn to articulate a defense of what they knew from Scripture to be true. Over the course of the semester, we would seek first to understand how God's word applied to issues, then how to respond to popular—but false—unbiblical arguments in the culture. And through frequent papers and in-class discussions, students would develop the ability to communicate these views effectively and persuasively, even among those who did not share our biblical worldview.

Learning to share and defend biblical truth is a key element of the ACU educational experience. Students are challenged to develop these skills in their major. And this focus drives our new CORE curriculum.

In the Fall of 2014, we launched our distinctive general education curriculum: *The CORE: Christian Liberal Arts for Cultural Transformation*. The ACU CORE is unique within American higher education and seeks to reclaim the liberal arts for the Christian tradition. Led by our faculty, students consider and discuss the great ideas of human history within the biblical worldview framework and use this rich understanding of the human experience to transform culture with the truth of God. And through the CORE, our students gain a solid understanding of who they are and what God has called them to do and be. The program uses a cohort-based, living-learning model; all students in a major take their CORE courses together, ensuring a strong social bond over their college years.

The program begins with the first-year experience, featuring two courses that introduce students to the ACU community and provide biblical worldview training. After that, students take four humanities courses during their sophomore and junior years. The courses span human history, from the dawn of time through today. Students read and discuss original texts to consider how human beings in other times and cultures understood their world and answered the big questions of life—about God, about what it means to be human, about purpose and meaning, about truth, beauty, justice and goodness.

Former Seattle Pacific University President Phillip W. Eaton, citing Fuller Theological Seminary President Richard Mouw, reminds us that the end goal of Christian higher education is not just to produce students who can think critically:

> Who among us as educators would ever say we do not need to continue to promote critical thinking?... Learning critical thinking should be part of any student's intellectual formation.
>
> "But the critical thinking thing must be a moment—a necessary exercise—in the service of a larger process," Mouw says. "And the larger goal is not simply to produce critical thinkers, but to equip persons who are faithful to the truth of the gospel. Some of us must engage in critical thinking in order to be effective in encouraging God's people to be faithful, both to the biblical message and to all that is good and worthy in the Christian traditions that we have received."
>
> We need critical thinkers for our society to flourish. This is a competency we must provide for our students. But our powerful culture of suspicion can easily lead us to suppose that critical thinking is the end goal of education.... But along with critical thinking, we must reach the "larger goal" of affirming—of trusting—our Christian story.[2]

So it is that ACU's CORE curriculum is designed to teach students to think critically in the context of the truth about who God is and who we are as His creation. As the number of young people who embrace a truthful, biblical understanding of the world has declined, it is more vital than ever that ACU graduates be able to forcefully and confidently defend the truth of the gospel among a generation, to paraphrase Judges 2:10, that doesn't know God.

CHAPTER FIVE

Arizona Christian University shall: *Teach students to…use technology effectively, develop interpersonal skills, and pursue personal and professional ethics through biblical literacy and integration.*

It would be easy to assume that training students to use technology effectively on the one hand, and to develop interpersonal skills on the other, are somehow in conflict. In reality, they are two sides of the same coin—and that coin pays the admission price to personal and professional success.

Without question, most students today need little help obtaining proficiency in the use of technology. They have been weaned on it since childhood. They don't know a world without Netflix, emojis, selfies, hashtags and the ability to ask your phone to magically draw you a living map to your next destination.

But proficiency in technology and using technology effectively are not necessarily the same thing. In particular, we see this with students who fail to understand that every self-revelation, every angry or cruel thought, every weak moment or irresponsible comment they have reflexively posted or tweeted will one day be visible to potential employers, potential spouses—university administrators!—and ultimately, to the rest of the world.

Through ACU's social media policy, we try to help our students gain an understanding of appropriate use of social media in the context of our Christian faith. This is not a question of freedom of speech. Paul put it this way in 1 Corinthians 10:23: "I have the right to do anything, you say—but not everything is beneficial. I have the right to do anything—but not everything is constructive." In addition, students at ACU sign a statement that they will abide by our community covenant, which includes behavior on social media.

Prospective ACU students risk having scholarship and admission offers rescinded due to Twitter or Instagram posts that are profane, vulgar, offensive, racially insensitive, or otherwise ungodly and unbiblical. Past and current ACU students have faced student discipline issues for similar posts.

Before posting or tweeting, as followers of Christ we should think through this reminder from Ephesians 4:29: "Do not let any unwholesome talk come out of your mouths, but only what is helpful for building others up according to their needs, that it may benefit those who listen."

These principles which should control our spoken words, also apply to words we use on social media because they reflect what is in our heart. As Jesus told us: "The good man out of the good treasure of his heart brings forth what is good; and the evil man out of the evil treasure brings forth what is evil; for his mouth speaks from that which fills his heart" (Luke 6:45). James expands on these principles in his letter to the church:

> For we all stumble in many ways. If anyone does not stumble in what he says, he is a perfect man, able to bridle the whole body as well. Now if we put the bits into the horses' mouths so that they will obey us, we direct their entire body as well. Look at the ships also, though they are so great and are driven by strong winds, are still directed by a very small rudder wherever the inclination of the pilot desires. So also the tongue is a small part of the body, and yet it boasts of great things. See how great a forest is set aflame by such a small fire! And the tongue is a fire, the very world of iniquity; the tongue is set among our members as that which defiles the entire body, and sets on fire the course of our life, and is set on fire by hell. For every species of beasts and birds, of reptiles and creatures of the sea, is tamed and has been tamed by the human race. But no one can tame the tongue; it is a restless evil and full of deadly poison. With it we bless our Lord and Father, and with it we curse men, who have been made in the likeness of God; from the same mouth come

CHAPTER FIVE

both blessing and cursing. My brethren, these things ought not to be this way (James 3:2-10).

These are principles we should take to heart every time we get ready to post or tweet!

To be successful in a technology-centered world, you need not only to understand how to use technology effectively, but also to gain the ability to navigate interpersonal relationships successfully. Dr. Marcia Y. Cantarella is an author and former administrator at Princeton University and New York University who writes for *The Huffington Post*. In her article "The Good News and the Bad News about College Students and Technology," she writes:

> In academia there is now the drive toward MOOCs. These massive open online courses can be taught by brilliant scholars, but you lose the connection to those scholars in real time. One of the key aspects of the college experience is learning how to interact with people of all kinds. *This is an essential workplace skill.* The professor is like the boss. You have to know what makes him/her tick and how to relate to a person in authority. The students who do best in college have strong relationships with faculty....
>
> Those who would propose that the college experience can be replaced fully by technology do not understand that learning is an interactive and social process. *For those going to college in late adolescence they are engaging in a transitional period of maturation. For those going to college to prepare for careers, they must build networks and resumes along the way. A purely technologically driven college experience, employers tell us, will not deliver the skills that make for good leaders, productive colleagues, or worthy stewards of any endeavor. Those skills involve working with other people.* Enforced classroom etiquette or taking on team projects or service learning are all good ways to engage students in activities in real time and

real life. It is important to read facial expressions and body language. You can't do that in a MOOC (emphasis added).³

Use of technology and growth in the ability to connect interpersonally are both important parts of the ACU educational experience, and our programs of study are designed to facilitate development in both. In a post-COVID pandemic world, the ability to use technology to learn and to connect will become even more vital. At ACU, even as we provide online degrees and the ability of students to attend classes remotely while other students are simultaneously attending in-person, we will always prioritize the necessity of effective interpersonal connection.

Growth in personal and professional ethics through biblical literacy and integration is the most unique and transformative element of the ACU Christian liberal arts education available at ACU. The report of the Liberal Arts Task Force summarized the goals of our new curriculum this way:

> It is with this desire to educate the whole person and transform culture with truth, as well as the mission to provide a biblically-integrated education that prepares its graduates to serve the Lord Jesus Christ, that Arizona Christian University approaches its liberal arts curriculum. The University does recognize that vocational training and skill development is important and can and does take place within its academic offerings, but the University's liberal arts core is dedicated to faithfully developing the whole Christian person for a life of service to others, not simply to a potential job, career, or employer. To that end, Arizona Christian University's liberal arts curriculum is grounded in the following principles:
>
> a) A liberal arts curriculum grounded in the Christian faith will help the student *theologically*, guiding their understanding of God.

b) A liberal arts curriculum grounded in the Christian faith will help the student *spiritually*, cultivating a personal relationship with Christ, giving them a greater sense of purpose.

c) A liberal arts curriculum grounded in the Christian faith will help the student *personally*, developing their understanding of their humanness.

d) A liberal arts curriculum grounded in the Christian faith will help the student *socially*, revealing the importance of faith for society at large.

e) A liberal arts curriculum grounded in the Christian faith will help the student *intellectually*, exposing them to a wider palate of educational experiences.[4]

Many students are seeing the transformational effects of a Christian liberal arts education in a biblical worldview context. As one student put it in a semester-end review:

> This semester has been so monumental for me.... The beauty that came from this class was that it reinstated everything that I believed but backed it up with more support and more evidence ... I am leaving this course with so much more knowledge and a better understanding of a Christian worldview but also other worldviews.... I feel encouraged and empowered to be able to share ... I have an understanding and a boldness to not just sit on this knowledge but ... share it.[5]

We live in a time of profound and transformational change, fueled by information technology. Training for a particular job could be effective, unless your career path is based on a vocation that technology will soon make obsolete. I'm sure horse-and-buggy manufacturers felt great about their future until the automobile was invented. A corporate career at Blockbuster Video or the local cable company looked pretty good until Netflix and streaming services came along.

Here is the thing: the ability to think critically and communicate effectively, combined with a solid set of personal and professional ethics that contribute to workplace integrity and a strong work ethic, are skills and abilities that cannot be replaced by technology. They prepare any college graduate for a wide variety of career possibilities. Combined with our emphasis on entrepreneurialism and internships, ACU graduates will be prepared to adapt to changing circumstances and bring value to any workplace environment. We are seeing that with many recent ACU graduates, who have moved ahead quickly in careers because of their ability to think well, communicate clearly and adapt to ever-changing circumstances.

We read that the average college graduate today will have seven different careers in the workplace. It's hard to nail down exactly where that data comes from, but what data is out there seems to confirm at minimum a high degree of "job-hopping" that is increasing among millennials. According to the Bureau of Labor Statistics, the average person has 10.8 different jobs (not necessarily careers) between ages 18 and 42.[6]

After graduating from college, my Dad spent close to 30 years at one company, Motorola, Arizona's largest employer for decades. It barely has an Arizona presence today. Other than a starter job at Hughes Aircraft and a brief detour to American Express, he basically moved up the ranks at one company from his mid-20s until he retired.

I feel like I've had a pretty stable career in many ways, but when I look back, I realize that, compared to my Dad, it's not even close to as stable. Here's what I've done:

1. Professional sportswriter (during college), four years
2. Attorney for a national nonprofit legal organization, one year
3. Judicial clerk for a federal appeals court judge, two years
4. Executive director of a national nonprofit legal organiza-

CHAPTER FIVE

tion, five years

5. President of a state-based, nonprofit ministry, 10 years
6. Candidate and Republican nominee for Governor of Arizona, one year (FYI, this "job" did not pay well, or at all actually)
7. Non-profit consultant and attorney in private practice, four years
8. President of Arizona Christian University, 10 years as of Fall 2020

Compared to recent and current college graduates and what I see happening in their careers already, my own job history may one day by contrast look as stable and consistent as my Dad's did to me.

But no matter what comes at our students in their career, they will be well-prepared, not just by a strong skill set but also by the deep hope and optimism available to those who are well-grounded in their Christian faith. Excellent thinking and communication skills, in a Christian ethical context, will provide ACU graduates with a great foundation for a successful career.

The official seal of Arizona Christian University includes a citation from this passage from Romans:

> I appeal to you therefore, brothers, by the mercies of God, to present your bodies as a living sacrifice, holy and acceptable to God, which is your spiritual worship. *Do not be conformed to this world, but be transformed by the renewal of your mind, that by testing you may discern what is the will of God, what is good and acceptable and perfect* (Romans 12:1–2; emphasis added).

The change that occurs through the renewing of our minds in a Christian university setting lays the foundation not only for professional and career success but also for success in the home and in our community, and ultimately in the revitalization and transformation of culture.

Chapter Notes

1. Dr. Roden and her late husband Jim Roden have been two of the most significant leaders in ACU's history. Dr. Roden served as Education Department Chair and Academic Dean, and she led various other key initiatives at the school for more than 20 years. Today Dr. Roden is a member of the ACU Board of Trustees and has been honored by the University with the naming of the Shelly Roden School of Education at ACU. Jim Roden was the founder of a business called ProChem, and together the Rodens have been among the school's most significant and generous financial supporters.
2. Richard Mouw, "Critical Thinking," *Fuller Theological Seminary President's Blog*, June 18, 2007, quoted in Phillip W. Eaton, *Engaging the Culture, Changing the World, The Christian University in a Post-Christian World* (Downer's Grove, IL: IVP Academic, 2011), 148.
3. Dr. Marcia Y. Cantarella, "The Good News and the Bad News about College Students and Technology," *The Huffington Post*, August 20, 2013, https://www.huffpost.com/entry/the-good-news-and-the-bad_2_b_3780192.
4. Report of the Liberal Arts Task Force, Arizona Christian University, June 3, 2013, 10. The ACU Mission included here was later updated to reflect the adoption of the new liberal arts CORE.
5. Anonymous student survey response to first ACU Liberal Arts course, December 2019.
6. Jeanne Meister, "Job Hopping Is the 'New Normal' for Millennials: Three Ways to Prevent a Human Resource Nightmare," *Forbes*, August 14, 2012, http://www.forbes.com/sites/jeannemeister/2012/08/14/job-hopping-is-the-new-normal-for-millennials-three-ways-to-prevent-a-human-resource-nightmare/.

SIX

Arizona Christian University shall:
Provide opportunities for students to serve locally and globally, and promote a culture of lifelong commitment to servant-leadership.

> Jesus called them together and said, "You know that the rulers of the Gentiles lord it over them, and their high officials exercise authority over them. Not so with you. Instead, whoever wants to become great among you must be your servant, and whoever wants to be first must be your slave—just as the Son of Man did not come to be served, but to serve, and to give his life as a ransom for many.
> MATTHEW 20:25–28

As a new university president in the Fall of 2010, it didn't take long for me to face my first student protest.

I got wind of it from a staff member before it made its way to my office. I was told that a student petition was being prepared to protest an action the school had taken—an action I wasn't even aware of. I was told that several hundred students, a majority of the entire student population, had already signed the petition—including two of my own children who were attending the college.

When the petition finally arrived on my desk, it occurred to me that this protest was unlike any I had ever heard about at any university. It was an early indicator of the remarkable character and heart of our students.

The petition request was simple. Through an administrative scheduling oversight, our University's annual Day of Service had been eliminated from the spring calendar. The students were simply asking that the service day be restored.

Granting that petition and restoring our Day of Service was one of the easiest decisions I've made as a university president. And for many years, we would set aside one day when all classes were canceled and hundreds of students would fan out all over the Phoenix metropolitan area to serve in various missions and ministries, from homeless shelters to food kitchens to prison ministries to pregnancy resource centers and much more.

Today, as ACU has grown, we no longer have just one day dedicated to service. We now have service activities in the community happening weekly through our student leaders and athletic teams, along with some University-wide Day of Service opportunities. We always hear great reports about our students from the ministries and the community. And we also often hear of the significant effect this service requirement has on our students. Occasional grumbling about the mandatory service hours invariably transitions to a deep sense of accomplishment and joy through helping others.

I first saw the unique Christ-like heart of our students for service when I was a new adjunct professor at then–Southwestern College in the early 1990s. As part of a fundraiser, I purchased some hourly help with yardwork at our house. I'm not sure what I was expecting, but I know I didn't expect what I got. A young man who came to our residence and, in the heat of a warm Arizona day, spent hours doing intense yardwork without taking a break and without looking for any shortcuts. I had rarely seen such a work ethic among adults, let alone a college student.

Of course, many of our students today are involved daily and weekly in ministry in the community, and many serve in ministries at local churches. But there is truly something remarkable—and different—about college students at Arizona Christian University who

CHAPTER SIX

are "other-focused" in a way that is noticeable and rare in a younger generation so often characterized as narcissistic and self-focused.

I say *noticeable* because on many occasions when I interact with others in our community, I hear stories about our students, about their character and maturity and how different they are from students at other universities in their demeanor, attitude and selflessness. I have also received letters and emails from strangers who, while perhaps previously unfamiliar with Arizona Christian University, interact with our students at restaurants, hotels, even airports around the country and are so impressed they reach out to me with words of encouragement and gratitude.

Philippians 2:3-4 says: "Do nothing from selfishness and empty conceit, but with humility of mind regard one another as more important than yourselves; do not merely look out for your own personal interests, but also for the interests of others."

A few years ago, one ACU student with a heart for service began to wonder, "If this college were not here, would our neighbors even notice?"

Christina Strohmeyer had applied for a student life leadership position as director of community service, with a vision of forming work groups of students to serve the neighborhood through tutoring, after-school programs, visits for the elderly and yard work. Because yard work was the easiest place to start, students canvassed the neighborhood letting people know ACU student leaders were available to help. At the height of the Great Recession, even in the middle-class neighborhoods of north Phoenix, the needs were many.

They named it the "032 Project" because the zip code surrounding ACU back then was 85032. Over time, students began working with city officials to identify elderly couples, single parents and others who needed help maintaining their properties.

Today the community-service mindset reflected in the 032 Project is embedded in the culture of ACU, and hundreds of students still participate in work groups each month. This has continued to create goodwill for ACU in its new neighborhood in Glendale, because of the many individuals and families who are dealing with personal or financial struggles and need help maintaining their homes and yards.

After leaving ACU, Christina Strohmeyer lived and served in Ankara, Turkey, where she taught English as a foreign language, sharing the love of Christ with students from first grade to high school, mentoring missionary kids, and helping to teach children and lead worship at her local church. The passion for serving others that she brought to ACU and developed as a student continued in her life, as it does in the lives of so many who graduate from our University.

In addition to providing opportunities for local service and cultivating a commitment to servant-leadership among students, ACU also provides opportunities for students to serve overseas. From hurricane relief in Haiti to teaching English in Indonesia to baseball clinics and youth ministry in the Dominican Republic to building an orphanage and ministering to orphans in Liberia, ACU students have had many opportunities for overseas service.

Brant Nyhart is ACU's former director of admissions and is married to an ACU alum. He also founded Global Resource Group, a charitable organization that partners with overseas ministries to promote development and opportunity in indigenous communities around the world.

In early summer 2014, his team of nearly two dozen ACU students and staff returned from a successful trip to Liberia that involved ministering to orphans, continuing to assist in building an orphanage and surrounding infrastructure, and engagement by some public policy students with political leaders in Liberia regarding the need for development and economic opportunities in that war-torn nation.

They returned just days before an Ebola outbreak in Liberia, which provided unique local and national media opportunities to draw attention to the significant needs of that West African nation.

Nyhart explains why missions' opportunities are vital to students at ACU:

CHAPTER SIX

- Missions broaden students' view of who God is by providing them an opportunity to see God at work in a different culture, often in different ways than they might see Him at work at home. As students interact with Christians in other cultures, it changes their perspective of what's truly important in life and often acts as a remedy against materialism. They learn that Christ is all they need, just as He is all most believers around the world have.

- Missions provide students an opportunity to grapple with difficult, real-world issues and therefore better prepare them to be the future decisionmakers, creative thinkers, and change agents in the world—it better prepares them to transform culture with truth. It's one thing to read about global conflicts, but it's quite another to visit a region that's been torn apart by war and see the effects of poor governance and corrupt regimes. This firsthand experience is crucial to being able to offer solutions to these issues. Another way I would phrase this, is it forces students to live outside the bubble that many of them have been in before going on these trips.

- Missions provide students an opportunity to minister with Christ's healing power in some of the most hurting places on earth.

- Missions build bridges amongst diverse segments of the campus population, with students who otherwise wouldn't interact with each other in a normal context being forced to come together for the goal of the trip. This starts well before the trip with students spending time fundraising together months before departure. The relationships that are formed on these trips last and promote campus unity.

- Missions provide students a greater opportunity to hear from God. I've seen time and time again where students go on these trips and hear from God in very specific ways—such as a specific calling on their life or direction with a relationship. When all the noise of Western culture is stripped away, it becomes easier to hear from God.

Nyhart tells the story of a meeting where ACU students were addressing a group of Liberian pastors. They were meeting in the location of a new church, which was housed in the burned-out home of a former rebel leader in one of the slums of Monrovia. The shell of a building had no windows or anything to protect church members from the elements. As one of ACU's students spoke about genuine love from Romans 12, one of the local pastors raised his hands and asked, "How am I supposed to love someone who killed my friend during the war?"

"Talk about having to walk the gospel out in ways we're rarely confronted with," Nyhart relates. "I was not at all sure how our student would handle this, but she gave a great, Spirit-led response. She said that she herself, in her own power, would not be able to forgive or love such a person. However, she assured him that the Holy Spirit had the ability to change his heart toward that person and thereby allow him to extend forgiveness and genuine love."

Another ACU alumnus first went to Liberia with Nyhart's team following her senior year at ACU. She has been back twice more and has been instrumental in teacher training efforts in Liberia. Relationships formed through University-sponsored mission trips often extend beyond graduation and lead to lifelong commitments to ongoing missions work.

Every student at ACU will have opportunities to serve and will be challenged to begin following Jesus by "looking out for the interests of others."

Those "others" may be across the street or across the world, but

CHAPTER SIX

the opportunity to develop a commitment to servant-leadership is an important part of the Core Commitments and the transformative education available at Arizona Christian University.

SEVEN

~

Arizona Christian University shall:
...influence, engage and transform the culture with truth by promoting the biblically informed values that are foundational to Western civilization, including the centrality of family, traditional sexual morality, lifelong marriage between one man and one woman, and the sanctity of human life...

Arizona Christian University shall*...influence, engage and transform the culture with truth by promoting the biblically informed values that are foundational to Western civilization...*

In 1987 on the campus of Stanford University, a group of about 500 students launched a protest against the school's traditional Western civilization curriculum, chanting, "Hey, hey, ho, ho, Western culture's got to go!"[1]

It did, and it has. Stanford quickly replaced the requirement that incoming students—considered the academic elite from across America and around the world—learn about the very ideas that gave birth to the prosperity and intellectual freedom that made a Stanford education possible. The reason? Apparently, it was unfair to impose the ideas of a bunch of "dead, white men" like Plato, Socrates and Aristotle on a new, multicultural generation.

But ideas, of course, should be evaluated on their own merit, not based on the ethnicity or gender of their authors or the time frame in which they were articulated. The notion that ideas either have value or not based on the race or gender of the person speaking is a profoundly racist, sexist and utterly false notion. Ideas have consequences, and unlike people, not all ideas are created equal.

At universities across America, over the past half-century the study of the biblically informed ideas and principles undergirding Western civilization has been virtually eradicated. To the extent Western ideas are discussed, they are dismissed, denigrated or ridiculed. A focus on the ways Western civilization has failed to live up to its ideals is combined with a celebration of other cultures and the promotion of worldviews antithetical to the West.

Columnist Herbert London wrote in 2011:

> It is astonishing that those in the West are living through the near extinction of their civilization. For students in the academy today, the Western civilization history course, virtually a standard curriculum offering 30 years ago, has disappeared.
>
> This survey course covering classical antiquity to the present was the glue, the all-embracing narrative, that gave coherence to everything else the university taught. At the very least, students came away from this course with a partial recognition of their civilization and its monumental achievements.[2]

For a Christian university, it is vital to understand the role and influence of Christianity and biblical principles in establishing the values we embrace in Western civilization. These biblical values lay a foundation for good citizenship and demonstrate the applicability of the principles of God to every area of life. As Dr. Eaton puts it:

> So many of the significant values we enjoy as a Western culture—values that have made us a decent society, even in spite of our failures—values such as individual freedom, freedom to practice religion (any religion), liberty for all,

respect for human dignity, respect for women, equality, kindness, civility, care for the poor, personal rights, the rule of law, the right to elect our leaders and the separation of church and state—it is not too much to say that most of all this emerged out of the [Christian] faith tradition....

When we look at this list of personal, social and cultural values, we must, of course, appropriately focus on the many painful ways we have fallen short of these aspirations. But the only way of judging our failures is by the set of standards *informed by these very values*. We cannot lose sight of the fact that without Christian influence, these values have no authority to give them substance and force. And so it seems baffling that we are now trying frantically and forcefully to eliminate the influence of [Christians] from the culture in which we live. The warning here is that we just may lose the values that hold our lives together.³

We live in a fallen world, and of course we have often failed to live up to our ideals. But as *Newsday* columnist Cathy Young writes, self-criticism is itself a Western tradition: "Enabled by our freedom, [self-criticism] is a strength that has allowed us to correct once-rampant injustices. But...[the] strength becomes a weakness when idealistic young people decide that their culture is so rotten it is not worth defending or preserving."⁴

And of course, that is exactly what has happened in America. We have systemically convinced the last few generations of Americans—through the public schools and universities of our country, along with popular media—that the values and principles of Western civilization and of America are not only flawed, but evil and destructive.

As a result, our culture is rejecting foundational principles that are time-tested and founded on biblical truth. That is why Arizona Christian University seeks to "influence, engage, and transform the culture with truth by promoting the biblically informed values that are foundational to Western civilization." We seek to remind students of the biblical truth that informs Western values so they can bring their influence to engage and transform a culture running headlong away from God and His principles.

The attacks on Western civilization have accelerated dramatically in recent years. The full-throated public embrace of socialism and attacks on liberty and economic freedom by politicians and protesters alike have not been seen since the end of the Cold War and the West's defeat of the Soviet Union and its satellite states. A recent outpouring of atheistic, secular left-wing ideologies in our country bears another similarity to its predecessors in other nations—with its commitment to eradicating free speech and desire to "cancel" and even criminalize opposing viewpoints. This totalitarian impulse is worthy of Nazi book-burners and Chinese internet censors, but unworthy of liberty-loving Americans.

One of the most disturbing elements of the civic unrest and violence that took place in the summer of 2020 was the way in which organizations embracing Marxism and anti-biblical, anti-family worldviews were able to co-opt peaceful protests about racial injustice, sometimes turning them into anti-American and anti-Christian violent revolutionary events. Protests that began to express legitimate and justified outrage over the unjust deaths of George Floyd and others at the hands of police were transformed by radical, ungodly organizations into explicit attempts to essentially overthrow the country and tear down Western civilization.

ACU stands fully in support of the biblically informed values of Western civilization. These values include equal justice under law, opposition to discrimination and commitment to civil rights for all. People of all races came together in 2020 to speak up against racism, injustice and unequal treatment under the law. As Christians who "hunger and thirst for righteousness," the passion for equality and justice is God-given. We recognize as a nation that we sometimes still fall short in our aspirations to treat everyone equally, and we want all of our people to be safe and feel safe. We want everyone to know that

CHAPTER SEVEN

of course it is true that every Black life matters; we know as Christians that every life is created in the image of God.

At Arizona Christian University—a community of followers of Jesus Christ that is significantly more diverse than the general population of Arizona—there should never be any doubt—there is no room for racism, injustice or unequal treatment based on race. We speak consistent biblical truth on these issues in chapel and in the classroom year after year and will continue to do so. These are principles we have consistently acted on through our admissions and recruiting process and through expectations for student conduct in our community, backing up our principles with actions, not just words.

In America, our laws and Constitution are designed to protect the life, liberty and property of everyone equally, and we must continue to work to protect these basic human rights and principles of justice. These founding principles as a nation are biblical, brilliant and worth defending; they represent our greatest aspirations. But our greatest failing has been our inability to fully live up to the hopes and dreams represented by those founding principles.

As Dr. Martin Luther King proclaimed in 1963: "I have a dream that one day this nation will rise up and live out the true meaning of its creed: 'We hold these truths to be self-evident, that all men are created equal.'"[5] More than 150 years ago we fought a bloody civil war to vindicate those principles and bring an end to slavery. More than 50 years ago we ended segregation and passed breakthrough civil rights legislation. We continue to "rise up" and yet we have not fully arrived.

So it is that when clear injustice occurs in front of our eyes, as it did with George Floyd and others in 2020, it shocks the conscience. The dream seems even further away.

We grieve every Black life lost through unwarranted police shootings and every Black life lost through violence and chaos in our cities. As Christians, we also grieve every Black life lost through abortion, which systematically targets Black children at much higher percentages than other races. We pray for peace, safety and justice for all, and the protection of innocent life.

In our community at Arizona Christian University, we believe unity and reconciliation will come through shared faith in the finished work of Jesus Christ to redeem us all from sin. At ACU we have intentionally sought to create a diverse community of Christ followers who are totally united around biblical truth and Jesus' command to "love one another."

I believe the students and community at Arizona Christian University represent the best of what is possible. I see such a longing among this generation of young people to do something significant, to be part of a great movement that will make history. The passionate and peaceful protests we are seeing are rising up from that God-given, biblical cry of the heart for justice and righteousness.

God in His infinite wisdom can bring good out of evil, hope from despair, and love out of hate. I believe the students, faculty and staff of ACU can lead the way in biblical, God-honoring unity through our shared relationship with Jesus Christ, in whom "there is no distinction … for the same Lord is Lord of all" (Romans 10:12).

We saw that in the fall of 2020, when ACU's community came together #UnitedinPrayer for an end to racism, injustice and unequal treatment under the law. As a community of Christians, we can do things in response to injustice that the world cannot—most importantly, ask the God of the universe for help! We know that God can do more than we can do in our human efforts, but so often forget to ask. So, on Sept. 11, 2020, several hundred members of the ACU community came together to pray. To ask God to forgive us of our sins, enable us to love one another, forgive one another, and move forward in unity and peace. We asked God to bring healing and reconciliation to our land. Together, students, faculty, staff and administration read the following pledge:

> Acts 17:26 teaches us that from one man—one race, one blood—come all the peoples and nations of the world. The students, staff, faculty and administration of Arizona Chris-

tian University stand #UnitedinPrayer for an end to racism, injustice and unequal treatment based on race. We mutually pledge to "love one another" (John 13:34) as brothers and sisters in Christ without regard to race and ethnicity. At ACU, we seek to demonstrate to the world that unity and reconciliation are possible through shared faith in Jesus Christ.

Students, faculty, staff and administration join together at ACU to pray for an end to racism and injustice at a #UnitedinPrayer rally on September 11, 2020, at Arizona Christian University.

What we have done at ACU, and what the vast majority of peaceful protesters have done to protest injustice, stand in stark contrast to individuals and even some organizations who are seeking to essentially overthrow Western civilization.

Those people and organizations have been looking to burn down cities, kill police officers, and overthrow Christian values of fatherhood, family, economic freedom and traditional sexual morality. Those ungodly purposes are the stated goals of some organizations who are exploiting racial injustice issues as a cover for their take-down of the biblical values that undergird Western civilization.

Sadly, even some Christian leaders have embraced a social justice movement that includes unbiblical critical race and social theory instead of a biblical worldview. As Scott David Allen, president of Disciple Nations Alliance and father of an ACU graduate, writes in his excellent new book, *Why Social Justice is Not Biblical Justice: An Urgent Appeal to Fellow Christians in a Time of Social Crisis:*

> Ideological social justice is dangerous because it is false. It is building a culture of hatred, division, a false sense of moral superiority, and a false understanding of justice. A culture where truth is replaced by power, and gratitude by ingratitude. A culture where everyone seeks out opportunities to be aggrieved and put on the mantle of the victim. A culture where people don't take responsibility for their lives, but instead blame all their problems on others. A culture of sexual libertinism and personal autonomy, where "sexual desire is the center of human identity and dignity." A culture where your identity is wholly defined by your tribe, and your tribe is always in conflict with other tribes in a zero-sum competition for power.
>
> In this culture, there is no "love your neighbors," much less "love your enemies." There is no grace. No forgiveness. No humility.[6]

Allen explains that on every major philosophical question—from "who we are" to "what is our fundamental problem as human beings,"

CHAPTER SEVEN

"what is the solution to the problem" and "how do we know what is true?"—the answers provided by the ideological social justice movement are in opposition to the biblical worldview.[7] In fact, social justice ideology is rooted in the class structure provided by Marxism—an atheistic philosophy that ignores God's creation of individuals in His image, and instead divides the world between oppressors and the oppressed. For Marx, it was worker vs. capitalists; for the social justice Marxists, the oppressors are white heteronormative males and the oppressed are people of color, women, sexual minorities and others. But social justice ideology completely denies the biblical view of human nature, the purpose of life and the nature of truth.

Most destructively, social justice ideology denies the truth that we all sin and fall short of the glory of God, and that we all can be saved if we call upon the name of the Lord. Instead, the problem is defined as oppressive power structures; salvation is not needed by victims and not available to oppressors except partially, but only if they confess their complicity in oppression by virtue of their race and gender while pledging support for the revolution.

That is why some of the organizations ostensibly created to fight against racism have unrelated and unbiblical calls for the destruction of the family and attacks on fatherhood. Yet the destruction of the God-ordained institution of the family, and the absence of loving fathers in the home—these are some of the clearest contributors to increased likelihood of participation in substance abuse, crime, self-harm, poverty and violence. These organizations supposedly fighting racism not only attack the traditional family, but also support an unbiblical, immoral and destructive agenda promoting sexual immorality. Many of these organizations also funnel donations to abortion advocacy, even though the big-money abortion industry since its racist founding has disproportionately attacked Black communities. These Marxist organizations also attack economic freedom and free markets, which have created the very opportunities so many minorities and immigrants have used to escape poverty and dependency and achieve a level of freedom and prosperity unparalleled in human history.

For all of these reasons, while ACU will continue to stand strongly against racism and injustice, ACU cannot be a part of any social justice organization or movement that promotes principles in opposition to the biblical worldview as reflected by our Core Commitments, including the centrality of family, marriage between a man and a woman, free markets and economic freedom, and a defense of the biblically informed values that are foundational to Western civilization.

The values described in this section of Arizona Christian University's Core Commitments are not political. They are biblical. They flow from ACU's historic understanding of the authority of the Bible and reflect our desire to recognize God's calling to engage all parts of culture with biblical truth.

Certainly, the application of biblical truth does not end when we consider policies related to government and public policy. Biblical principles apply not only to our personal lives but also to our family relationships, our relationships in the body of Christ through our church, and our relationships within the community and also with our civic government. There are clear biblical principles that apply to leaders and to governments. But while the principles might have political implications, they remain biblical principles.

Indeed, it would be odd to claim that God is omnipotent (all powerful) but lacks any influence over this one area of life we dismiss as "political." In fact, the Bible tells us that all worldly and governmental authority is not only given by God but also exists to serve Him. In describing the exalted Christ, Paul writes: "For by Him all things were created, both in the heavens and on earth, visible and invisible, whether thrones or dominions or rulers or authorities—all things have been created by Him and for Him" (Colossians 1:16).

This is earth-shattering for those who believe Christians and biblical truth have no role to play in the political arena. Paul is telling us that Christ not only created government—"rulers and authorities"—

but that the purpose of government is to serve Him! The logical conclusion from such a broad statement is that those of us who know God and His ways should bring those principles to bear on government. It also seems obvious that some Christians should be willing to serve God by taking positions in government.

We've already noted how over time Christians have lost influence at major American universities. But nowhere have Christians been told more vociferously that their ideas are invalid and illegitimate than in the arena of politics. Yet nothing could be further from the truth.

As we discuss biblical principles, some of which have applications or implications that could be considered political, keep in mind how important it is for Christians to understand what God's word teaches about these issues and to bring these biblical principles to bear. The most important aspect of this section of the Core Commitments is not any potential policy implications. It is the opportunity to understand and embrace a biblical worldview on issues being discussed and debated in our culture today.

Arizona Christian University shall…*influence, engage and transform the culture with truth by promoting…[t]he centrality of family, traditional sexual morality and lifelong marriage between one man and one woman.*

As we discuss emotionally charged issues of human sexuality, family, marriage and divorce, we all have a choice to make—whether to embrace what God says about family, marriage and sexuality, or whether to just go along with the tide of current thinking.

Choosing to follow God in these areas will require moral courage. Choosing the Word over the world—even in America—is becoming costlier each day. Especially in this area of sexual morality, the politically correct cancel culture is working to make traditional biblical perspectives forbidden. Almost every week now it seems a public person—a CEO, a broadcaster, a business owner, an athlete—is excoriated, forced to apologize or fired for speaking biblical truths regarding human sexuality. But these moral truths have formed the bedrock of our civilization for thousands of years, including the entirety of American history.

Scripture teaches us to "do all things without grumbling or disputing; so that you will prove yourselves to be blameless and innocent, children of God above reproach in the midst of a crooked and perverse generation, among whom you appear as lights in the world" (Philippians 2:14–15).

We have an obligation to speak truth and to serve as lights to those around us. Generations of Americans coming into adulthood today have grown up surrounded by cultural lies regarding marriage, family and sexuality. They will need to hear the truth, not from my generation but from their peers, who understand and can lovingly and compassionately articulate God's best plan for all of us.

The family is the fundamental building block of civil society. God ordained and defined both marriage and the family, beginning in the book of Genesis. As theologian and Phoenix Seminary professor Dr. Wayne Grudem points out, "From beginning to end, the Bible has a very positive view of bearing and raising children. In fact, the very first recorded command to human beings was the command to bear children."[8]

God declared in Genesis 1:27–28 that He created man in His own image, "male and female he created them," then blessed them and instructed them to "be fruitful and multiply and fill the earth and subdue it."

Throughout Scripture, children are viewed as a blessing from the Lord and a natural consequence of marriage (Psalm 127:3–5; Malachi 2:15; 1 Timothy 5:14). Parents are responsible for teaching children the principles of God (Deuteronomy 6:4–7), and when children listen to their parents' instruction (Proverbs 1:8, 6:20), they can lead happy, productive and long lives (Ephesians 6:1–4).

And here is the simple truth: the family is formed through God's plan that sexuality be expressed *only* within the safety of a lifelong marriage commitment between one man and one woman.

So that was and is the plan for expression of human sexuality. Sexual activity within marriage is designed to provide both intimacy and the possibility of procreation. Male and female bodies complement each other and naturally work together to create new life. Through their children, the husband and wife literally come together and form "one flesh" (Genesis 2:24).

Today there is much debate about the definition of marriage. The Supreme Court in 2015 purported to settle the issue through a decision that manufactured out of thin air a "right" to same-sex marriage. But a moral wrong must never be accepted as a civil right.

Jesus provided us with the true definition of marriage: "Have you not read that He who created them from the beginning made them male and female, and said, 'For this reason a man shall leave his father and mother and be joined to his wife, and the two shall become one flesh?'" (Matthew 19:4–5).

The marriage relationship is so foundational and significant that the Bible uses it as a picture of the relationship between Christ and the church (Ephesians 5:22–32).

The definition of marriage quite obviously predates its recognition by law and by governments. Until recently, American law always recognized marriage as the union of one man and one woman. Previous assaults on the definition of marriage were turned away by the U.S. Supreme Court. Upholding a law prohibiting polygamy, the Supreme Court in 1885 said:

> Certainly no legislation can be supposed more wholesome and necessary in the founding of a free, self-governing commonwealth…than that which seeks to establish it on the basis of the idea of the family, as consisting in and springing from the union for life of one man and one woman in the holy estate of matrimony; [the family is] the sure foundation of all that is stable and noble in our civilization.[9]

Following Jesus today in America means choosing to turn away from so many sexual sins that are commonplace, rampant and accepted in our culture. In just a few generations, we have moved from a culture that understood and embraced a biblical view of sexuality to a culture that actively celebrates choices that lead only to devastation, disease, heartbreak and brokenness.

In a fallen world, all of us are sexually broken in various ways. All of us have faced and will face sexual temptation outside the bonds of male-female marriage. And thanks to the advance of technology and degradation of our culture, opportunities for immoral conduct are omnipresent. They are as close as your smartphone or laptop computer.

Those who are tempted by same sex attraction or pornography, premarital sex or adultery have the same choice we all face in a fallen world—will we choose to obey God or obey our flesh? God is really, really, *really*, clear on this—like, over and over again! In 1 Thessalonians 4: 3-5, we read: "For this is the will of God, your sanctification; that is, that you abstain from sexual immorality; that each of you know how to possess his own vessel in sanctification and honor, not in lustful passion, like the Gentiles who do not know God."

Adultery, homosexuality, pornography, sex trafficking, incest, cohabitation, premarital sex, pedophilia—all can be grouped under the general Scriptural banner of "sexual immorality." Paul tells us to "[f]lee sexual immorality. All other sins a person commits are outside the body, but whoever sins sexually, sins against their own body" (1 Corinthians 6:18). Both Old and New Testament passages clearly identify sexual conduct that is outside the boundaries God provides within male-female marriage.[10]

Current misinterpretations of Scripture that attempt to justify or excuse what God clearly calls sin are easily refuted.[11] The only question is whether we will believe and follow what the Bible teaches.

Whether we choose to obey or not, no Christian should be confused about what God asks of us in these areas. In my own life and

CHAPTER SEVEN

in the lives of friends, family and fellow churchgoers over the past several decades, without question the deepest regrets we have are the direct consequence of decisions we've made contrary to the will of God relating to sexual morality, marriage and family. God gave us the gift of human sexuality. It was His idea, and it is a good gift! He did not place limitations on the gift of sexuality in order to torture or frustrate us. He did so in order to protect an undefiled marriage bed: "Marriage is to be held in honor among all, and the marriage bed is to be undefiled; for fornicators and adulterers God will judge" (Hebrews 13:4). He did so to protect our hearts by enabling lifelong pleasure, joy and intimacy to occur safely with one person, rather than experience the pain of broken sexual relationships. He did so to protect our bodies from diseases that occur through promiscuity. He did so to protect children from being raised without any sense of permanent love and stability in their home. Sexuality was given for our good, and the boundaries around it are also for our good.

The radical change in our culture over the past 30 years to a wholesale embrace and celebration of sexual immorality has been breathtaking in both its scope and speed, and has made it much more difficult for young people today than in the past. Almost overnight, we threw out thousands of years of moral teaching on marriage and sexuality, with no thought given to the human wreckage we are creating.

A 2015 comedy film starring Amy Schumer called *Trainwreck* is the story of a woman who tries to take control of her life through ongoing promiscuity that she initiates, believing that she is liberated and free and enjoying herself. She was taught this philosophy by her unhappy, selfish and adulterous father. Her life is a series of drunkenness and one-night stands, until she meets a man who seems to care about her. Only then does she begin to recognize the deep sadness and shame of her conduct. The film itself is vulgar and profane, and in no way written from a biblical worldview. Even so, it reflects the sad truth of a life given over to sexual immorality—there always comes a point of reckoning with God's truth. Late in the film, she tearfully looks at her boyfriend and sadly says, "I'm broken." At one point she asks him, "What's wrong with you that you want to be with me?"

Because the truths of God are written on our hearts, no matter how much the world and the culture today tells us to just "go for it" sexually, there will come that day of reckoning; that moment of quiet, somber and sad recognition of our depravity before a holy God. Even in our hyper-sexualized culture, there will eventually come a moment when we recognize, like Amy Schumer's character in *Trainwreck,* that we are broken. We are all sexually broken.

Whether it is through constant stirring up of lust through obsessive pornography usage, or sexual conduct with someone of the same gender in violation of the laws of nature, or sexual conduct with person after person after person, without a commitment to lifelong marriage, everyone will reach that quiet moment of despair and shame.

The good news is this: despite living in a culture that surrounds us daily with sexual temptation, God's grace is sufficient. When we agree with Him about our sexual sin, when we repent and turn back to God, He makes all things new and brings healing to our lives.

We have one example from Scripture of Jesus directly encountering sexual immorality: the story of the woman caught in adultery (John 8:1-11). Jesus first points out the hypocrisy of the judgmental religious leaders, urging whoever is "without sin" to throw the first stone. As the men drift away, Jesus turns to the woman: "Jesus said to her, 'Woman, where are they? Did no one condemn you?' She said, 'No one, Lord.' And Jesus said, 'I do not condemn you, either. Go. From now on sin no more'" (John 8:10-11).

We can learn so much from this short encounter. When it comes to sexual immorality, Jesus is the only one who can offer us grace and forgiveness from sin, including sexual sin. As we encounter those who struggle with sexual sin, we should recall our own failings rather than feel superior or judgmental.

But at the same time—and this is important—He upholds the standard of sexual morality. He encourages her to "sin no more."

CHAPTER SEVEN

When we uphold biblical standards of sexual morality against a cultural onslaught, we are showing love to those caught in a spiral of hopelessness and brokenness. We can point people to a place of hope and healing, as they embrace God's design for human sexuality and freedom from the bondage of sin.

King David is described as "a man after God's own heart," despite falling into the sin of adultery with Bathsheba. His beautiful prayer of repentance in Psalm 51 reminds us that despite our brokenness, we can speak truth with compassion to those around us:

> Have mercy on me, O God, according to your unfailing love;
> according to your great compassion blot out my transgressions.
> Wash away all my iniquity and cleanse me from my sin.
> For I know my transgressions, and my sin is always before me.
> Against you, you only, have I sinned and done what is evil in your sight;
> so you are right in your verdict and justified when you judge....
> Create in me a pure heart, O God, and renew a steadfast spirit within me.
> Do not cast me from your presence or take your Holy Spirit from me.
> Restore to me the joy of your salvation and grant me a willing spirit, to sustain me.
> Then I will teach transgressors your ways, so that sinners will turn back to you.

The sanctity of human life

> For you formed my inward parts; you knitted me together in my mother's womb. I praise you, for I am fearfully and wonderfully made. Wonderful are your works; my soul

knows it very well. My frame was not hidden from you, when I was being made in secret, intricately woven in the depths of the earth. Your eyes saw my unformed substance; in your book were written, every one of them, the days that were formed for me, when as yet there was none of them (Psalm 139:13–16).

As a parent, I can tell you the most extraordinary moments of my life involved the births of each of our eight children. The notion that God would allow us—flawed, sinful, scared, inadequate humans—to participate and cooperate with Him in the miraculous creation of new life is beyond my comprehension. I will never forget that moment of recognition, as a first-time father, when I realized that God used me and my wife to create a brand new human soul—for whom we are now responsible! For me, it was at once an overwhelming, terrifying and exhilarating moment.

As the passage from Psalm 139 indicates, God creates life in the womb and plans out each person's life before a single day is lived outside the womb. The Bible supports a reverence for the sanctity of human life that is distinctively Christian. Multiple passages testify to the humanity of the unborn and newly born child:

- In Exodus 1, the Hebrew midwives ignored an edict from Pharaoh to kill newborn male babies because they "feared God" (Exodus 1:15–21).

- In Luke 1 we discover that John the Baptist "leaped for joy" while in his mother's womb when he came into the presence of the preborn Jesus: "And when Elizabeth heard the greeting of Mary, the baby leaped in her womb. And Elizabeth was filled with the Holy Spirit, and she exclaimed with a loud cry, 'Blessed are you among women, and blessed is the fruit of your womb! And why is this granted to me that the mother of my Lord should come to me? For behold, when the sound

CHAPTER SEVEN

of your greeting came to my ears, the baby in my womb leaped for joy'" (Luke 1:41–44).

- In Exodus 21 we see the criminal code reflects an understanding that killing a human child in the womb is considered murder: "When men strive together and hit a pregnant woman, so that her children come out, but there is no harm, the one who hit her shall surely be fined, as the woman's husband shall impose on him, and he shall pay as the judges determine. But if there is harm, then you shall pay life for life, eye for eye, tooth for tooth, hand for hand, foot for foot, burn for burn, wound for wound, stripe for stripe" (Exodus 21:22–25).

In ancient times child sacrifice, abortion, child abandonment and infanticide were commonplace but not universal. Christians changed that nearly 2,000 years ago and affected a cultural change in favor of life that only unraveled in America in the past few decades. In his book *Evangelical Ethics,* John Jefferson Davis gives examples from ancient China, Greece and Rome to conclude:

> Abortion was a common practice in the ancient world.... [But] early Christianity resolutely opposed abortion, which was common in the Roman world.... [A] manual of Christian morals and church affairs from the first century stated, "Thou shalt do no murder...thou shalt not procure abortion, nor commit infanticide...." Very similarly, the "Epistle of Barnabus" stated, "Thou shalt not procure abortion, thou shalt not commit infanticide."[12]

In the second century, the Christian apologist Athenagoras wrote, "How can we kill a man when we are those who say that all who use abortifacients are homicides and will account to God for their abortions as for the killing of men. For the fetus in the womb is not an animal, and it is God's providence that he exists."[13]

Davis goes on to trace the next few centuries, from Tertullian to the Council of Ancyra in 314 AD, to the writings of Augustine, through the Middle Ages, to conclude that Christian opposition to abortion and euthanasia was consistent and formed the foundation of Western thought on these issues. That understanding of abortion was reflected in the culture and laws of Western nations including the United States, where abortion was illegal except when the mother's life was threatened in all 50 states until 1967—when I was 4 years old.[14]

Knowing human beings are created in the image of God, and that God is the author of life, Christians have always engaged culture in defense of the dignity and worth of every human life. Despite the legalization of abortion in America through Supreme Court decree in 1973, the consistent, compassionate witness of many different Christian faith traditions has brought new attention to the humanity of the unborn. Public opinion polls reflect newfound support among young people for protecting life in the womb. Advances in ultrasound technology and the ability to perform surgery on babies in utero is making it more and more obvious that the life of an innocent human being is at stake. So it is that Christians continue to seek an opportunity for the Supreme Court to overturn its barbaric decision in *Roe v. Wade*—a moral atrocity similar to the Supreme Court's 1857 *Dred Scott* decision to deny citizenship to Blacks. Because *Roe*, like *Dred Scott*, violates the foundational principles of our country by denying personhood to babies until birth, it too must ultimately be overturned.

News reports in 2015 about the sale of preborn children's body parts by Planned Parenthood, America's largest abortion provider, have reminded Americans about what actually occurs during an abortion—the dissection of a human being. They have also brought renewed attention to the racist roots of Planned Parenthood's founder Margaret Sanger, who sought to establish clinics in predominantly African American communities. Dr. Alveda King, niece of the Rev. Dr. Martin Luther King Jr., has argued that the higher percentage of abortions that occur in the African American community are a form of genocide caused by the eugenics promoted by early advocates of abortion.

CHAPTER SEVEN

Followers of Jesus—through the joyful acceptance of children, embrace of adoption, opposition to abortion and abortifacients, and reverence and care for the elderly and infirm—continue to demonstrate their support for the sanctity of human life in a manner that is influencing the culture back toward truth.

Arizona Christian University shall… *influence, engage and transform the culture with truth by promoting the biblically informed values that are foundational to Western civilization, including:*

- *compassion for the poor,*
- *a biblical understanding of human nature, an understanding of God's purposes for limited government, personal, economic, and religious freedom, free markets, capitalism, and property rights, natural law, the original meaning of the Constitution, and judicial restraint,*
- *international human rights and the advancement of freedom throughout the world.*

Compassion for the poor

Whoever oppresses a poor man insults his Maker, but he who is generous to the needy honors him.

PROVERBS 14:31

More than 300 passages of Scripture speak to our obligation as Christ-followers to care for the poor. A quick review of these passages leaves a very strong impression for any serious follower of Jesus. Here are some key principles:

- We should give to the poor anonymously without drawing attention to our generosity (Matthew 6:2–4).
- God considers our treatment of the poor and hungry a

reflection of the way we treat Him (Matthew 25:34–46; Proverbs 14:31).

- We should guarantee that the poor receive equal justice under the law and are not taken advantage of due to their poverty (Exodus 23:6; Proverbs 31:9).

- Our willingness to surrender our earthly possessions to help the poor is a demonstration of the priorities in our hearts (Luke 12:32–34).

- Those who give to the poor and help those in need are blessed, will be repaid by the Lord, and demonstrate both love for their neighbor and for God (Proverbs 14:21, 19:7).

The Christian perspective on poverty is very different from a Darwinian "survival of the fittest" approach or a utilitarian philosophy that would view the poor as a drain on society. If only the fittest and most useful survive, the poor and needy will be outcasts and given little opportunity for growth, productivity and opportunity for advancement.

Cultures built on worldly philosophies will inevitably look for ways to push the poor to the edge of society.

The biblical worldview, recognizing the dignity and worth of every human life, sees beauty and significance in even the most marginalized members of society. Jesus was our example in the compassionate way He treated sinners, strugglers, beggars, the sick, the infirm and those who were least financially able to contribute to ministry. While Jesus noted in passing that we would always have the poor among us, on many occasions He asked His followers to feed the hungry, clothe the naked, and otherwise meet the physical needs of the poor.

While there is no question about our obligation to the poor as Christians, there are many questions about the most effective and biblical approach to addressing the needs of the poor. The Scriptural admonitions regarding giving to the poor are directed exclusively at individuals. By contrast, the Scriptural guidance for civil government is only that government, through its justice systems, must treat the poor fairly. A rich man and a poor man appearing in court should be treated equally. There is no Scriptural support for the notion that governments have the authority to redistribute wealth. To the extent government policies take earnings away from some citizens—under penalty of jail time if you don't pay taxes—and give money to the poor, they rob the wealthy of the virtue and blessing of following God's call to be generous.

In America in recent decades, the failure of the body of Christ to take care of the poor and needy has led to massive governmental intervention in the form of a "war on poverty." But after nearly a half-century of this "war," the same percentage of Americans are poor now as were poor before we began spending trillions of dollars to supposedly eradicate poverty.

A groundbreaking book by theologian Dr. Wayne Grudem and economist Dr. Barry Asmus explained why the War on Poverty was destined to fail. In *The Poverty of Nations: A Sustainable Solution*, the authors identified well-intentioned principles that do not alleviate poverty, and these principles apply to individuals as well as nations. These mistaken policies include continuing to provide donations (welfare), which robs the poor of the ability to achieve human happiness through earned success; redistribution of wealth from the rich to the poor; and blame-shifting regarding the cause of poverty.[15]

Regarding ongoing welfare, Grudem and Asmus write:

> ...[T]here is no thought in the Bible that poor people would become recipients of gifts of money, year after year, or would become dependent on such gifts. The only exceptions were people who were completely unable to work due to permanent disabilities.... In the New Testament, Paul rebuked those who were "idle" (1 Thess. 5:14, 2 Thess. 3:7), stipulating, "If anyone is not willing to work, let him not eat" (2 Thess. 3:10).[16]

The authors go on to explain that requiring work is not unkind or harsh and that the opportunity to earn success in the workplace is a gift from God, who gave work to Adam in the Garden of Eden even before sin entered the world. Regarding redistribution, Grudem and Asmus note:

> ...the Bible does not support the idea that governments should forcibly take from the rich simply because they are rich and give to the poor (beyond basic needs) simply because they are poor.... Nowhere does the Bible teach that it is the responsibility of the government to attempt to equalize incomes between the rich and the poor.[17]

Recent political rhetoric in America has sought to demonize wealthy people by appealing to jealousy and envy. But Scripture teaches us that covetousness is a sin; we are not to covet the possessions and wealth of our neighbors (Exodus 20:17). At the same time, some Christians have misappropriated the story of early Christians in Acts 2—selling possessions and sharing everything in common—as a justification for socialism. But the voluntary sharing of resources among a fellowship of brothers and sisters in Christ is entirely different. We are called individually as Christians to be generous and share with those in need. So often it is Christians who have attained wealth who not only take care of the needs in the local body of Christ, but fund ministries and advance the gospel. Indeed, Arizona Christian University would not exist but for the sacrificial giving that comes from followers of Jesus. The tuition and fees that come from students only pay a portion of the costs of a private college education.

Voluntary and virtuous charity within the body of Christ, however, is far different than a mandatory, government-imposed redistribution of wealth scheme that punishes achievement. There is no virtue in being forced by law to surrender resources you have earned—or be sent to jail. And while God ordained government for certain limited purposes, as Grudem and Asmus note above, mandating equality of

CHAPTER SEVEN

wealth is not a legitimate or biblical purpose of government.

Our compassion for the poor should motivate us to engage with the poor in productive ways and not attempt to shift our responsibilities to an inefficient and heartless government program through wealth redistribution. Ultimately, government poverty programs are destined to fail because, as former President George W. Bush used to say in explaining his faith-based initiatives, "Government may put food on your table but it can't put hope in your heart."

When Jesus told us the story of the Good Samaritan, we should note that the Samaritan was good because he personally and voluntarily chose to help the bruised and beaten traveler with his own resources. He did not leave the traveler by the side of the road and head to the local seat of government to lobby for bigger welfare programs and government health care.

Compassion for the poor is a biblical obligation for followers of Jesus Christ. Christians in the West for more than 2,000 years have been building hospitals, homeless shelters and food kitchens, and forming organizations like the Red Cross and the Salvation Army, because they have taken seriously God's call to love our neighbor as ourselves. At ACU, we are committed to teaching Christians to channel their God-given compassion for the poor into productive and helpful ministry activity that provides genuine help to the needy. Many students regularly participate in various service projects to benefit those in need as part of our spiritual formation programs; we hope and pray this will be an ongoing way of life for ACU graduates as they continue to demonstrate God's compassion for the poor.

A biblical understanding of human nature, an understanding of God's purposes for limited government, personal, economic and religious freedom, free markets, capitalism, and property rights, natural law, the original meaning of the Constitution and judicial restraint...

> ...[F]or all have sinned and fall short of the glory of God....
> ROMANS 3:23

It might be easy to dismiss this list of values reflected in ACU's Core Commitments as a set of political perspectives, without recognizing that they are foundational principles reflective of the biblical worldview of America's Founding Fathers. The fact that these fundamentally American values have become controversial today is a direct consequence of our failure to explain and teach these principles in the schools and universities of America. Indeed, universities have been on the cutting edge of attacking a biblical worldview as it relates to government and culture.

For Arizona Christian University to prepare students to effectively transform culture with truth, there must be an understanding of how the biblical worldview encompasses God's plan for *limited government*, and how and why biblical values were instrumental in the formation of the government and the Constitution of the United States.

We should not be surprised that Scripture speaks to every area of human existence, including providing a blueprint for the appropriate role of government.

Years ago, I was in a public debate at the Phoenix Country Club before hundreds of Arizona leaders regarding the First Amendment and the supposed "wall of separation" between church and state. I was debating a member of the clergy who was also a professor at Arizona State University.

I briefly walked through the historical evidence of Christianity's role in the founding of America and in structuring our government. When I finished, the ASU professor said, "Well, Len is basically right about the history. But we know better now."

Sadly, our departure from these foundational principles may be evidence that "we know better" to some public intellectuals, but the reality is quite the opposite—just look around at what's happening today. The reality of the challenges facing America and the world as a result of abandoning a biblical perspective provides a great deal of

CHAPTER SEVEN

evidence to the contrary.

Fundamentally, the Founding Fathers' biblical worldview caused them to be skeptical of power. They understood, as the passage above declares, that man's nature is fallen and prone to sin and corruption. As Lord Acton would put it a century later, "power corrupts; absolute power corrupts absolutely." The Founding Fathers sought to separate and diffuse power in the structure of government precisely because of their scriptural understanding that individuals need accountability. As James Madison wrote in Federalist No. 51, in support of ratifying the Constitution:

> If men were angels, no government would be necessary. If angels were to govern men, neither external nor internal controls on government would be necessary. In framing a government which is to be administered by men over men, the great difficulty lies in this: you must first enable the government to control the governed; and in the next place oblige it to control itself. A dependence on the people is, no doubt, the primary control on the government; but experience has taught mankind the necessity of auxiliary precautions.[18]

So the Founding Fathers divided the power of government—federal power offset by state power—and three branches of government that provide checks and balances to each other.

None of these steps are necessary if you believe man is inherently good. In that case, you would simply set up a government and choose the best person to run it, allowing that person to have absolute power. Of course history has shown that whether absolute power was exercised by a king or queen or by tyrannical dictators like Hitler, Stalin and Mao, the results in terms of human rights abuse, corruption and murder of the innocent speak for themselves.

In my debate with the ASU professor, he pointed out that God and the Bible are not mentioned in our Constitution (other than the date at the end of the document—in the "Year of our Lord" 1787). He was correct. But I responded by citing from memory Isaiah 33:22: "For the Lord is our judge, the Lord is our lawgiver, the Lord is our King, he will save us," pointing out that our three branches, judicial, legislative, and executive—the very structure of our federal government—are based directly on a passage of Scripture describing the governing attributes of Almighty God. This was news to him, and to the audience. But it was not a surprise to our Founding Fathers, who structured our Constitution that way quite deliberately.

Because of our biblical worldview in America, we framed a Constitution that limited the power of government. Today, however, with the passage of time, we have forgotten what we set out to do and we see an increase not only in government power and control over our lives but also an increase in corruption and abuse of power. Christians have the opportunity and obligation to work to restore our founding, biblical perspective on limited government.

From a biblical perspective, and according to our Constitution, the role of national government is simple—keep order (1 Timothy 2) by providing for the national defense and punishing evildoers (Romans 13:4), while administering justice fairly (Jeremiah 22:13; Psalm 11:11). Taxes are appropriately collected from the population to cover these purposes (Romans 13:6–7). Much of what government does today is well beyond its constitutional scope and beyond what Scripture would indicate is appropriate, leading to massive overtaxation that penalizes achievement, overspending and borrowing that undermines sovereignty.

The Founding Fathers, whether Christians or not, all embraced a biblical worldview and structured a government for a society that embraced a biblical worldview. As John Adams said, "Our Constitution was made only for a moral and religious people. It is wholly inadequate to the government of any other."[19] His son, John Quincy Adams, our sixth president, was more explicit: "From the day of the declaration…they [the American people] were bound by the laws of

CHAPTER SEVEN

God, which they all, and by the laws of the gospel, which they nearly all, acknowledge as the rules of their conduct."[20]

Much ground has been lost, but it is important for Christians to recognize the foundations of our American government and to defend the *original meaning of the Constitution* against its usurpation by activist federal judges. So many deviations and distortions of our national purpose have been initiated by unelected judges, who are duty bound to interpret the law rather than rewrite it. There is a parallel here with interpretation of Scripture—at ACU we believe and teach that the Bible is inerrant and inspired, and the goal is to understand what God is trying to communicate. Some today start with a position on a certain issue and then read Scripture to buttress their argument. In the same way, some *judges* today want to reach a certain outcome before they begin, so they impose their modern interpretation of the Constitution on us rather than *restrain* themselves by determining how to apply the founders' principles to modern challenges.

The Declaration of Independence provides a ringing endorsement of *personal, economic and religious freedom,* but it is difficult for us today to reconcile these statements of principle with the grotesque travesty of human slavery at the time of the Founding. History is clear that many Founders believed these statements were hypocritical in light of the South's insistence on maintaining slavery in southern states; but with the success of the American Revolution against England hanging in the balance, the Founders chose to compromise.

But the language of the Declaration was not to be denied—the "self-evident" truth that "all men are created equal" was vindicated less than a century later at great cost through a bloody Civil War. The principles were true and eternal, but the application has always been inconsistent and subject to the sins and selfishness of fallen human beings. It took yet another century before a Christian pastor, Dr. Martin Luther King Jr.—who moved the American people again and again with his rhetorical appeals to our common Christian values and sense of justice—cited the words of the Declaration in his "I Have a

Dream" speech on the Washington Mall that finally fueled passage of the Civil Rights Act of 1964.

Despite limited application in the 18th Century, with women denied the vote and African Americans enslaved, the written principles of our founding were just and biblical and need to be recovered and elevated. The Founders of America were fighting for personal, economic and religious freedom, all of which are under assault in the United States again today. The soaring language of the Declaration of Independence—with its citation to the laws of nature and nature's God—has inspired generations of freedom-loving people to come to the United States or to initiate change in their own countries.

The United States is often envied and frequently criticized for failing to live up to its own stated virtues. Yet, as discussed in the Introduction, to much of the world America truly has become that "city on a hill" (Matthew 5:14) depicted by John Winthrop in 1630 as he prophetically anticipated the influence of a future nation in this New World. When young protesters filled Tiananmen Square in China in 1989 to protest that brutal, totalitarian regime's human rights abuses, they chose the Statue of Liberty as their symbol. The protests were crushed by the regime, proving again that governments with no foundation in Scripture, with no limits and no checks and balances on sinful men, have no motivation to do anything other than stifle fundamental freedoms and liberties in order to preserve their power and position. China continues to suppress freedom of all kinds and subjugate its people today—another reminder that we should be so grateful for the freedoms we have in our nation, rather than take them for granted.

Personal freedom and a form of ordered liberty restrained by Christian virtue was what the Founders believed would enable the new nation to succeed with its experiment in representative self-government. The Apostle Paul, in discussing our freedom in Christ, notes that "all things are lawful, but not all things are profitable" (1 Corinthians 10:23). In America we have great personal freedom, with

CHAPTER SEVEN

opportunity to move around as we wish, to enter into relationships as we wish, to pursue our dreams—all things unavailable in much of the world today. However, our liberty is put at risk when we refuse to govern ourselves. John Adams said, "The only foundation of a free Constitution is pure Virtue, and if this cannot be inspired into our People in a greater Measure…they will not obtain a lasting liberty."[21] We see that in extreme examples. When a handful of terrorists hijack airplanes and fly them into buildings, the rest of us lose the freedom to board airplanes without invasive searches. In a broader sense, limited government is not possible when people choose at a widespread level to violate the Ten Commandments and walk away from God's principles for marriage and family. Government naturally grows to provide the police and prosecutors and social welfare agencies to address social breakdown, and by its very nature this growth in government places new limits on our personal liberties.

We still have *religious freedom* today, although recent attacks on Christians who refuse to participate in activities that violate their conscience are raising questions about our culture's commitment to this historic liberty—the "first freedom" under our Constitution's Bill of Rights. The restrictions on church gatherings imposed during the pandemic were both historically unprecedented, and in my view, blatantly unconstitutional. Without taking a position on whether churches should gather, it should be clear they had a right to. The First Amendment states that the government can make no law "prohibiting the free exercise" of religion, but that's exactly what some executive orders did during the pandemic. Shockingly, some lower courts upheld total bans on religious gatherings. It is my belief that as these cases make their way up the appeal process, the right for people to gather for religious activities will ultimately be vindicated.

We are told in the Old Testament to "choose this day" who we will serve (Joshua 24:15). Without getting into a theological debate about predestination—we either choose Christ or he chooses us, or maybe both—without a doubt our ability to publicly exercise our faith is very much affected by our society's commitment to religious freedom. Christian efforts at evangelism are generally characterized by love, compassion, acts of service and speaking the truths contained in God's word. Some evangelists can be verbally confrontational. But in America, we have the right to free speech and free exercise of religion. Sadly, in other parts of the world today, citizens in some countries are being ordered to either convert to Islam or face beheading. Other nations prohibit any religious activity that is not sanctioned or allowed by the government. That such barbaric restrictions on the right of conscience exist in our modern world is an offense to God and to man.

Economic freedom is preserved in America through our historic commitment to *free markets, capitalism, and property rights,* all of which are supported by a biblical worldview.

In *The Poverty of Nations,* Grudem and Asmus lay out not just the economic but also the theological case for free markets and capitalism, with frequent citations to Scripture.[22] In recent years I've noted a dramatic increase in scholarship that provides a clear moral and biblical foundation for the virtues of work, the free enterprise system, and private property.[23]

There has been a growing recognition that from the moment God assigned work to Adam in the Garden of Eden, he was providing the first man with the opportunity to use his creative gifts. As a man created in the image of a creative God, Adam was able to bring order and value out of the earth in order to bless God and ultimately provide for his family.

Proverbs 13:4 confirms the value of diligent work, "The soul of the sluggard craves and gets nothing, while the soul of the diligent is richly supplied," and Proverbs 14:23 declares, "In all toil there is profit, but mere talk tends only to poverty."

Jesus told a parable of the talents—primarily to deliver a spiritual message—yet the parable indicates that those who are industrious in increasing wealth will have greater opportunities and rewards (Matthew 25:14–30). Paul indicated that those who don't work won't eat, emphasizing the virtue in hard work and the rewards associated with our labor (2 Thessalonians 3:10).

Economic systems that attempt to punish success and reward laziness find no support in Scripture, nor do systems that attempt to expand government control by depriving citizens of their ownership of *private property*. Without private ownership of property, many of the primary laws given to us by Almighty God—the Ten Commandments—make no sense. After all, if no one can own anything, then why have a prohibition on stealing? If everything is publicly owned and belongs to everyone, there is no need to prohibit coveting your neighbor's house and property (Exodus 20).

The Founders also recognized that God's law was clear to believers and unbelievers alike, and expected our legal and governmental system to reflect the principles of God even while protecting the freedom to worship as you please. This understanding of the "natural law" came directly from Scripture: "When Gentiles, who do not have the law, by nature do what the law requires, they are a law to themselves, even though they do not have the law. They show that the work of the law is written on their hearts" (Romans 2:14–15).

The Founders believed the laws of nature were universal, known to all citizens, and expected the systems of government to act consistently with the natural law.

International human rights and the advancement of freedom throughout the world.

To our knowledge, Arizona Christian University is the only university in the United States to teach a class called "American Exceptionalism."

America is not exceptional in the sense that our people are more worthy or deserving or favored in some way than citizens of other nations. America is exceptional because of the ideas on which it is founded—the biblically informed values of Western civilization we have been discussing in this chapter.

Nowhere is this more clear than in America's historic commitment to serving other nations, not only through financial help and foreign aid but also by frequently coming to the assistance of other countries during humanitarian crises, and more significantly, by being willing to lay down our lives to combat injustice and tyranny in other nations.

At its root, our willingness to help defend international human rights and advance freedom throughout the world is based on Jesus' admonition to "love one another." We are told first to love the Lord our God, but the Second Commandment is: "'You shall love your neighbor as yourself.' There is no other commandment greater than these" (Mark 12:30–31).

Nothing is more disconcerting than the sentiment heard frequently these days that America should ignore injustice in other lands. Had that sentiment prevailed prior to World War II, we might still be dealing with a deadly and powerful Nazi regime. Had that mindset prevailed during the Cold War, much of Eastern Europe would still be under the oppression of atheistic Communism.

Whatever your view of the wisdom of our original engagement in recent wars, efforts to combat radical Islamic terrorism at its source in Afghanistan, and to dethrone a cruel dictator in Iraq who threatened his own people and his neighbors, were unquestionably militarily successful in providing hope and opportunities for freedom. In 2004, the people of Afghanistan flocked to the polls to vote. I will never forget the pictures of Afghani women who had not been allowed to attend school, and who had suffered under constant oppression, smiling and holding up their inked thumbs to prove they had cast votes in a national election for the first time. Sadly, it takes a generation or more to establish principles of democracy in a nation. With the withdrawal of allied troops, those countries will continue to battle to prevent a return to Islamic extremism that will limit their hopes and dreams of freedom.

As we benefit from freedom and prosperity, we have a moral obligation to help those who still suffer under tyranny and oppression. I

CHAPTER SEVEN

am reminded of the words of Psalm 94:16–23:

> Who rises up for me against the wicked? Who stands up for me against the evildoers?... Can wicked rulers be allied with you, those who frame injustice by statute? They band together against the life of the righteous and condemn the innocent to death. But the Lord has become my stronghold, and my God the rock of my refuge. He will bring back on them their iniquity and wipe them out for their wickedness; the Lord our God will wipe them out.

Historically, America has been willing to go to war to liberate other nations. Unlike many other nations, we haven't stayed as conquerors, but instead have established principles of self-government for other nations, then allowed them to chart their own destiny. Time will tell whether America will continue to have the capacity or desire to love the people of other nations enough to set them free.

CHAPTER NOTES

1. Richard Bernstein, "In Dispute on Bias, Stanford is Likely To Alter Western Culture Program," *New York Times,* January 18, 1988, http://www.nytimes.com/1988/01/19/us/in-dispute-on-bias-stanford-is-likely-to-alter-western-culture-program.html.
2. Herbert London, "How Western Civilization Disappeared From College Campuses," *Manhattan Institute for Policy Research,* http://www.manhattan-institute.org/html/miarticle.htm?id=7713#.VEKq0Pl4pcQ.
3. Phillip W. Eaton, *Engaging the Culture, Changing the World* (Downers Grove: IVP Academic, 2011), 87–88.
4. Cathy Young, "In defense of 'dead white males'," *Boston Globe,* March 8, 2013, http://www.bostonglobe.com/opinion/2013/03/08/defense-dead-white-male-studies/PyVWxltFsjzPPzVrwF536O/story.html.
5. Martin Luther King, Jr., "I Have a Dream," Address Delivered at the March on Washington for Jobs and Freedom, August 28, 1963, https://kinginstitute.stanford.edu/king-papers/documnets/i-have-a-dream-address-delivered-march-washington-jobs-and-freedom.
6. Scott David Allen, *Why Social Justice is Not Biblical Justice: An Urgent*

Appeal to Fellow Christians in a Time of Social Crisis (Grand Rapids, MI: Credo House Publishers, 2020), 195.
7 Ibid., 56-58.
8 Wayne Grudem, *Politics According to the Bible: A Comprehensive Resource for Understanding Modern Political Issues in Light of Scripture* (Grand Rapids, MI: Zondervan, 2010), 245.
9 Murphy v. Ramsey & Others, 144 U.S. 15, 45 (1885).
10 Scriptural admonitions include: "You shall not commit adultery" (Exodus 20:14); "For this reason God gave them up to dishonorable passions. For their women exchanged natural relations for those that are contrary to nature; and the men likewise gave up natural relations with women and were consumed with passion for one another, men committing shameless acts with men and receiving in themselves the due penalty for their error" (Romans 1:26–27); "But sexual immorality and all impurity or covetousness must not even be named among you, as is proper among saints.... For you may be sure of this, that everyone who is sexually immoral or impure, or who is covetous (that is, an idolater), has no inheritance in the kingdom of Christ and God" (Ephesians 5:3, 5).
11 See generally Grudem, *Politics According to the Bible*, Chapter 7.
12 John Jefferson Davis, *Evangelical Ethics: Issues Facing the Church Today*, 2nd ed. (Phillipsburg, NJ: P & R Publishing, 1993), 118–19.
13 Ibid.
14 Ibid., 139–140.
15 Wayne Grudem and Barry Asmus, *The Poverty of Nations: A Sustainable Solution* (Wheaton, IL: Crossway Books 2013), 72–74.
16 Ibid., 73.
17 Ibid., 79.
18 James Madison, Federalist No. 51, in *The Federalist Papers*, (New York, NY: Cambridge University Press 2007), 251.
19 John Adams to the Officers of the First Brigade of the Third Division of the Militia of Massachusetts, 11 October 1798, in *Revolutionary Services and Civil Life of General William Hull*, ed. Maria Campbell and James Freeman Clarke (New York: D. Appleton and Co., 1848), 265–6.
20 John Quincy Adams, "An Address, Delivered at the Request of the Committee of Arrangements for Celebrating the Anniversary of Independence, on the Fourth of July, 1821," Archive.org, accessed 10/23/2014, http://archive.org/stream/addressdelivered00adamiala/addressdelivered00adamiala_djvu.txt.
21 John Adams to Zabdiel Adams, in *Letters of Delegates to Congress*, vol. 4 (Washington, DC: Library of Congress, 1976–2000).
22 See generally Grudem and Asmus, *The Poverty of Nations*, Chapter 6, "The

CHAPTER SEVEN

Moral Advantages of the System: A Free Market Best Promotes Moral Virtues."
23 See, for example, the Acton Institute for the Study of Religion and Liberty, www.acton.org and The Institute for Faith, Works and Economics, www.tifwe.org.

EIGHT

~

Arizona Christian University shall:
Prepare students to be leaders of influence in their community, state, nation, and world—through the church, the family, business, government, education, health care, media, the arts, and every area of society.

> You are the salt of the earth, but if salt has lost its taste, how shall its saltiness be restored? It is no longer good for anything except to be thrown out and trampled under people's feet. You are the light of the world. A city set on a hill cannot be hidden. Nor do people light a lamp and put it under a basket, but on a stand, and it gives light to all in the house. In the same way, let your light shine before others, so that they may see your good works and give glory to your Father who is in heaven.
>
> MATTHEW 5:13–16

Since the time of Christ more than two millennia ago, followers of Jesus have influenced the world around them.

In 1926 a pastor in Los Angeles delivered a message that included a segment on the influence of Jesus, later titled "One Solitary Life":

> Here is a man who was born in an obscure village, the child of a peasant woman. He grew up in another obscure village, where He worked in a carpenter shop until He was thirty, and then for three years He was an itinerant preacher. He

never wrote a book. He never held an office. He never owned a home. He never had a family. He never went to college. He never put his foot inside a big city. He never traveled two hundred miles from the place where He was born. He never did one of the things that usually accompany greatness. He had no credentials but Himself. He had nothing to do with this world except the naked power of His divine manhood. While still a young man, the tide of public opinion turned against Him. His friends ran away. One of them denied Him. He was turned over to His enemies. He went through the mockery of a trial. He was nailed to a cross between two thieves. His executioners gambled for the only piece of property He had on earth while He was dying—and that was his coat. When he was dead He was taken down and laid in a borrowed grave through the pity of a friend. Nineteen wide centuries have come and gone and today He is the centerpiece of the human race and the leader of the column of progress. I am far within the mark when I say that all the armies that ever marched, and all the navies that ever were built, and all the parliaments that ever sat, all the kings that ever reigned, put together have not affected the life of man upon this earth as powerfully as has that One Solitary Life.[1]

Because Jesus—the Son of God—came to earth "and dwelt among us," the world is a different place. As we have seen, followers of Jesus Christ have not only shown others the path to reconciliation with a holy God and eternal life in heaven but have also made this world a better place in the here and now. As author C. S. Lewis once put it, "Aim at heaven and you will get earth thrown in. Aim at earth and you get neither."[2]

By focusing on the things of God, Christians have made the world a better place by bringing biblical truths to bear on individual lives and the broader culture, and ultimately forming a foundation for the values that gave birth to what we now refer to as Western civilization.

CHAPTER EIGHT

Christ followers for 2,000-plus years have fed the hungry, clothed the naked, cared for the poor, visited those in prison, cared for orphans and widows, and influenced individuals and nations with principles of righteousness and goodness. Christians have promoted personal conduct that demonstrates the influence of the Holy Spirit—love, joy, peace, patience, kindness, goodness, faithfulness, gentleness, self-control—conduct far removed from natural human tendencies, and conduct that has enabled civil society to flourish (Galatians 5:22–23). Followers of Jesus have gotten married, stayed married, and raised children in families that become the foundation of civic society and community. Christ followers have promoted integrity, self-sacrifice, love, compassion and justice. They have contributed to the welfare of those around them by building churches, orphanages, homeless shelters, food kitchens, schools, hospitals, universities and ultimately, civilizations.

Christians who have operated according to God's instruction have indeed been "the light of the world," and the world is a better place as a result.

Yet without question, in the past century Christian engagement and influence in the United States has diminished. This has occurred for two reasons—external forces who are hostile to God and Christianity have sought to remove biblical influence from our culture, while at the same time some Christian leaders have themselves determined that any attention to the culture is wasted energy.

Anti-Christian zealots like Madalyn Murray O'Hair and attorneys from organizations like the ACLU began in the 1960s—with the help of liberal, activist judges—to remove any vestige of Christian influence from the public sphere. They started by removing Bible reading and prayer from the public school system, escalated with attacks on prayer at civic and governmental events, and are culminating now with forced allegiance to new cultural norms on abortion and sexuality enforced by governmental decrees that force Christians to violate their conscience or be punished.

At the same time, our popular culture and our public education system have undertaken to whitewash Christian influence from any discussion of American history, while promoting the perspective that America is an evil nation that got rich exploiting slavery and the natural resources of other nations.

Sadly, many Christian leaders have contributed to the decline of Christian influence in the culture by embracing a mindset that because the return of Christ is imminent, we need to stop caring about the culture, stop caring about our communities, our nation, our institutions of civic life, and instead focus all of our attention on evangelism.

As discussed earlier, a commitment to evangelism—sharing the good news about Jesus and his sacrifice for our sins—is an essential and natural part of our relationship with Christ. But a commitment to evangelism does not require a withdrawal from culture. In fact, we are less able to share the gospel effectively when we are ignored, marginalized, or mocked by the broader culture.

Evangelism and cultural engagement are not "either/or" propositions. Best-selling author Eric Metaxas exposes the flaws in that perspective:

> Often we have engaged the culture—if it can be called that—only for the purposes of evangelism. We've sometimes acted as though "getting everyone saved" was the only real project we should be involved in, as though that would solve all of the other, larger cultural issues. Perhaps if we led enough people to faith—the upside-down McCulture, like a flipped kayak, would at some point suddenly right itself with a single Super-sized McSplash. But often we have not even cared about the culture at all. Many of us have thought that since the Lord would be returning around the year 1994–2000 at the latest—what did it matter if everything was going to Sheol in a handbasket? This is the standard *Dude-it's-all-gonna-burn theology*, which permits complaining about the

CHAPTER EIGHT

culture, but not doing anything about it—besides, of course, rescuing people *from* it before it all burns.

This tack has the double disadvantage of being unbiblical *and* not working. Indeed, it has backfired badly, because without Christians involved in it, the culture only got worse.[3]

That's what we've seen in recent decades. Many Christians pulled out of areas of influence in our culture—politics, media and the arts, business leadership, public education—or became afraid to speak up and share their convictions out of fear of being marginalized or blackballed. As a result, the culture got worse.

Lately, largely as a result of a rise in anti-biblical thinking on marriage and sexuality, with efforts to punish those who believe in Scripture, a defeatist mindset has set in even among Christian leaders.

At a gathering of Christian college presidents, I was stunned and disappointed by the seeming acquiescence of so many to such a recent and dramatic shift away from biblical perspectives on heterosexual monogamy and marriage as cultural norms. The discussion was about how to survive in the midst of cultural losses viewed as inevitable and permanent. The message was similar at a recent gathering of Southern Baptist pastors and leaders, where one news report said, "Speakers at the event said they understood they were on the losing end of the culture war on marriage."[4]

Recently I've also heard it described this way: We used to have the "home-field advantage" in our culture, but now we need to recognize that we are the "road team." The crowd and the referees are against us, and the home-field advantages we were used to are gone.

But these notions that we have "lost the battle over marriage" or that we have "lost the culture" are completely unbiblical. It would be as if Christians in 1857 had decided to give up fighting slavery after the Supreme Court issued its ruling in the *Dred Scott* case, saying in essence, "Well, we tried, but we've lost the battle over slavery."

To the extent these perspectives embrace defeatism or acquiescence in the face of evil cultural choices, they are simply not biblical.

They completely deny the ability of Jesus Christ to change hearts and minds.

To be blunt, I want the home-field advantage back. Christianity and Christian principles *should* be at the center of our culture. That would be better for everyone.

Given our eternal perspective, Christians, of all people, should take the long view of history and culture by recognizing that today's cultural trends are neither inevitable nor irreversible. In fact, history is filled with examples of Christians losing ground then regaining it. Certainly the history of the nation of Israel in the Old Testament involved God's people turning away from Him, turning back to Him, turning away and turning back. We have to remember that we are "not of this world," which means that we are not always called to victory, but we are certainly always called to engagement. President John Quincy Adams wrote, "Duty is ours, results are God's."[5] He was right. But there is zero possibility of regaining Christian influence in our culture if we retreat into bunkers and monasteries and hope the increasing anti-Christian totalitarian impulses will just leave us alone.

In his article "Trickle Down Culture," Metaxas describes the work of 19th-Century abolitionist leader William Wilberforce, who not only was evangelistic but also fought slavery and continually worked to bring Christian principles to bear on the world around him:

> Wilberforce and his friends had a monumental impact on the wider British culture, and on the world beyond Britain, because they succeeded not only in ending the slave trade and slavery, but in changing the entire mindset of the culture. What had been an effectively pagan worldview, where slavery and the abuse of human beings was accepted as inevitable and normative, became an effectively biblical worldview, in which human beings were seen as created in the image of God. The idea that one should love one's neighbor was brought into the cultural mainstream for the first time in history, and the world has never been the same.[6]

CHAPTER EIGHT

In recent decades in America, the departure of Christians from positions of influence in our culture has been profoundly damaging to Christians and non-Christians alike. When you reduce or remove Christian principles and ethics from Wall Street, from Hollywood and from Congress, the culture will change. And ours has, to the detriment of our families and children and of our civic life, peace and prosperity—and to the detriment of our "domestic tranquility," to quote the preamble to our Constitution.

But like Wilberforce, we should not accept these circumstances as the perpetual status quo.

At Arizona Christian University, it is our desire to help young men and women discover God's unique gifting and call on their lives, then prepare and equip them to be the best Christian leaders they can be in every area of influence in society.

God has a plan for each of us. "For we are his workmanship, created in Christ Jesus for good works, which God prepared beforehand, that we should walk in them," according to Ephesians 2:10.

God's plan is different and distinct for each follower of Christ, depending on the unique combination of attributes and abilities and gifts we have been given: "Now there are varieties of gifts, but the same Spirit; and there are varieties of service, but the same Lord; and there are varieties of activities, but it is the same God who empowers them all in everyone. To each is given the manifestation of the Spirit for the common good" (1 Corinthians 12:4–7).

In recent years, largely in response to the declining influence of biblical principles in American culture, a number of Christian leaders from a variety of theological backgrounds—beginning with the late Bill Bright of Cru (Campus Crusade for Christ) and Loren Cunningham of YWAM (Youth With A Mission)—have agreed that we need an effort to reengage spheres of influence within our culture.[7] All Christians should recognize the benefits of godly leadership in our culture. The Book of Proverbs tells us that "when the righteous increase"—or become influential or in authority—"the people rejoice, but when a wicked man rules, the people groan" (Proverbs 29:2).

Sometimes referred to as the Seven Mountains Movement, a number of groups like Scottsdale-based Pinnacle Forum, a national organization seeking to transform leaders in our culture, are dedicated to influencing leaders in the following mountains, or spheres, of cultural influence: religion, education, business, government, media, arts and entertainment, and family.

This is not some reconstructionist or dominionist theological movement about Christians trying to take over the world and thereby usher in the return of Christ. This is simply about Christians being "salt and light," engaging with culture, and seeking positions of leadership to help preserve liberties and promote values and principles that will cause all people to flourish. It's about our call to "seek the welfare of the city" (Jeremiah 29:7) at times, like now, when the influence of God's people has been diminished.

By design, Arizona Christian University offers degrees that prepare our graduates to move into these seven spheres of societal and cultural influence:

- Religion—through our Biblical Studies and Christian Ministries programs;
- Education—with the training of teachers through our Education degree;
- Business, including health care—through our Business Administration and Biology degrees;
- Government—through our Political Science, Pre-law and Criminal Justice programs;
- Media—through our Communication degree;
- Arts and Entertainment—through our Music degree and Film Studies programs;
- Family—through our Psychology and Behavioral Health degrees.

CHAPTER EIGHT

As Wilberforce demonstrated in England nearly two centuries ago, changing cultural norms require Christians to pursue leadership positions and then use their influence for godly purposes. Metaxas explains how members of the Clapham Circle—Wilberforce's collection of leaders who chose to live and work in the same area for ease of building community, planning, and prayer—held onto their positions of influence and used them for God's purposes:

> But the Clapham Circle were not mere culture warriors, trying to climb over the ramparts to take control, but rather were already insiders who knew how to behave like insiders, and who would do their best to change things from within. They knew how to move in their high circles of influence; knew the unspoken language of those circles; and knew when to push and when not to push and whom to ask about this or that, and whom not to ask. They looked and behaved like everyone else, except for their deep faith, so they were simultaneously insiders and outsiders. As we have said, they may well be the most "in the world, but not of it" network of people who ever lived. As "not-of-the-world" outsiders, it was vital they spend time together, encouraging and praying with each other. They were aware that they were also God's ambassadors and missionaries within the elite culture of their day, much as Joseph and Daniel in theirs. The Clapham Circle did all they could to maintain their places of power and influence, so long as it advanced the gospel, because their ultimate allegiances were not to the "world" in which they moved, but to the "not of-the-world" Kingdom, whose King they served.[8]

That is our desire for students at Arizona Christian University. I have used my influence in the community many times on behalf of ACU students who seek to be influencers in their generation and beyond, and I expect to do so many times in the future as the university grows in numbers and reputation. I see our faculty and staff doing the same. So we have ACU graduates, even recent ones, already moving into positions of leadership or preparing to do so. Pastors and seminary leaders, worship leaders at large churches, lawyers and law students at prestigious schools, doctors and medical students, educators, business owners, counselors, TV news reporters, police officers, government officials, and much more. As the years pass and this vision begins to be fulfilled—as we let our lights shine before the world—a network of ACU faculty, staff and alumni will have both the ability and obligation to help other Firestorm family members move into positions of influence in our culture, all for the purpose of transforming culture with God's truth.

Chapter Notes

1 James Allan Francis, *One Solitary Life* (1963), 1–7, http://www.bartleby.com/73/916.html.
2 C. S. Lewis, *Mere Christianity* (San Francisco: HarperSanFrancisco, Harper edition, 2001), 134.
3 Eric Metaxas, "Cultural Elites: The Next Unreached People Group," http://old.qideas.org/essays/cultural-elites-the-next-unreached-people-group.aspx?page=3.
4 Rachel Zoll, "Southern Baptists Tell Pastors: Hold the Line on Gay Marriage," Associated Press, October 28, 2014, http://www.apnewsarchive.com/2014/Southern-Baptist-meeting-presses-evangelical-leaders-to-stand-up-for-heterosexual-marriage/id-701a48a8b2e6428193f4c1c6a5aaa3e8.
5 William J. Federer, *America's God and Country* (Coppell: FAME Publishing Inc., 1994), 15, quoting David Barton, *The WallBuilder Report, Aledo, TX: Wall Builder Press, Summer 1993)*, 3, in reply to a question, 1828.
6 Eric Metaxas, "Trickle-Down Culture," *Christian Union*, October 3, 2014, http://www.christianunion.org/cu-today/18-christian-union/332-trickle-down-culture.
7 Christian leaders call this the "Seven Mountains Movement." Here is more information: http://www.christianpost.com/news/engaging-the-seven-mountains-of-culture-christians-urged-to-transform-culture-outside-of-church-walls-110491/.
8 Metaxas, "Cultural Elites," 1.

CONCLUSION

~

Arizona Christian University shall:
Be a leading conservative Christian liberal arts university.

Labels, like stereotypes, are often overbroad, inapplicable or inappropriate. But labels and stereotypes are typically based on some level of factual information, and they exist because we sometimes need and desire a shorthand way to quickly communicate basic descriptions of people and things.

So it is with Arizona Christian University. On first review, when we consider ACU's commitment to be a "leading conservative Christian liberal arts university," it would appear to pit two opposite perspectives—"conservative" vs. "liberal"—in the same label. But that's not correct.

Our commitment to teaching what is true, based on the authority of the Bible, provides context to this final element of our Core Commitments.

The notion of being a "leading" university really speaks to the idea that our desire is for ACU to produce graduates of influence for the cause of Christ, graduates committed to excellence in their academic discipline and their spiritual walk, graduates who will become leaders. As we seek year by year to improve every element of the ACU education for our students, to move toward excellence as an institution, our expectation is that ACU will become a national leader in producing graduates who will accomplish great things for the cause of Christ.

The combination of ACU's statement of faith for staff and faculty, our commitment to biblical inerrancy, and our statement of Core

Commitments would naturally cause us, in today's lexicon, to be considered a theologically and culturally "conservative" institution. And to some extent, that label would be accurate, in that—as has been described throughout this book—there are foundational values in Western civilization that are based on biblical truth that we believed should be *conserved*. At the same time, we note that conservative values in today's world are profoundly *countercultural*—which makes today's conservative Christian leaders the actual bold intellectual revolutionaries of this era.

At the same time, we have deliberately moved beyond our foundation as a small Bible college and are now in the process of becoming a great Christian liberal arts university. We have made a conscious choice to identify with the value and significance of a Christian liberal arts education, and that decision is changing both what we teach and how we teach it. Our approach to teaching now is designed to maximize our ability to engage our students with biblical truth, through a combination of larger classes and small groups, forcing critical thinking and ownership and growth in each individual student's faith commitment. And beginning in 2020, we will be the first Christian university that is actually measuring the progress our students make in thinking biblically about the world.

We believe a Christian liberal arts education is the most capable of producing leaders of substance, ability and character—leaders who can think critically and lead persuasively—leaders desperately needed in a culture gone astray.

When I think of the truths our culture has abandoned, and the subsequent destructive effect on our families and our civic institutions, I ask God to raise up a generation of Christian leaders who can bring the love of Christ and the truth of Christ to their generation in a way that will awaken their peers to the hope found in Jesus, and to the significance of a life lived well in obedience to God and his principles. I ask God to raise up leaders who will restore lives, repair families and civic institutions, and bring reformation and transformation to our

CONCLUSION

culture.

My prayer for the students of Arizona Christian University is from the prophet Isaiah, 58:11–12:

> The Lord will guide you always;
>   he will satisfy your needs in a sun-scorched land
>   and will strengthen your frame.
> You will be like a well-watered garden,
>   like a spring whose waters never fail.
> Your people will rebuild the ancient ruins
>   and will raise up the age-old foundations;
> you will be called Repairer of Broken Walls,
>   Restorer of Streets with Dwellings.

From the deserts and "sun-scorched" land of Arizona, I pray God will bring forth leaders from Arizona Christian University who will rebuild the ancient ruins of a Christ-centered culture, raise up the age-old foundations of Western civilization, and restore and repair the families and homes that are the building blocks of our culture. I pray God will continually guide our students as they transform culture with truth!

ABOUT THE AUTHOR

Len Munsil is an attorney and the sixth President of Arizona Christian University, serving since September of 2010. He was the 2006 Republican nominee for Governor of Arizona, and the founding President of The Center for Arizona Policy, the nation's largest and most influential state-based Christian pro-family organization. He was selected by the *Arizona Capitol Times* as one of the "2020 Leaders of the Year" in the area of Education. He and his wife, Dr. Tracy Munsil, an associate professor at Arizona Christian University, are the proud parents of eight adult children. Their expanding family now includes three sons-in-law, two daughters-in-law, and 10 grandchildren (and counting). The Munsils live in Phoenix, Arizona.

www.ingramcontent.com/pod-product-compliance
Lightning Source LLC
Chambersburg PA
CBHW050236120526
44590CB00016B/2117